JIN M0

QI GONG

AN ALTERNATIVE TECHNIQUE TO DEEP TISSUE MASSAGE THAT USES PRINCIPLES OF WORKING AND CONNECTING WITH THE BODY'S FASCIA, ENERGY, AND CORE, WHILE PROMOTING SAFE AND EFFECTIVE RESULTS FOR BOTH PATIENT/CLIENT AND PRACTITIONER

By **Val Nardo**, LMT, M.Ed., Ph.D., *retired*

Val Nardo

ISBN: 978-1-965408-08-7.

Acknowledgments

My wife Kathleen and daughter Eve have always been supportive of my endeavors and I wish to give special thanks to both of them for their support in my pursuit to start and finish, JIN MO QI GONG.

I wish to thank Clayton College of Natural Health for developing such a comprehensive, self-motivating educational program that provided the foundation and requirements for detailed research on the concepts of Natural Health. My life changed for the better because of my interest and my studies at Clayton College. Thank you, Clayton College, wherever you may be.

I would also like to thank Cross Country Education and HomeCEUConnection for providing me with the venues to develop and teach my massage therapy techniques.

Finally, may I continue to learn and serve my fellow humans in some worthwhile capacity.

Val Nardo

Table of Contents

Jin Mo Qi Gong

Foreword

In this book, I hope to share information accumulated over a period of seven-plus years of research, practice and seminar presentation in the field of massage therapy. In the summer of 2007, I became connected with Cross Country Education. This company provided continuing education training on a national level for massage therapists and other therapeutically related occupations. Immediately that summer, I was asked to develop a program for Cross Country Ed. dealing with the subject of "Deep Tissue Massage." At first, I was reluctant to pursue the subject of DTM because of my negative experiences with it, as well as my lack of knowledge of it. Then, as I began to evaluate this subject more closely, it became clear to me that there must be a better way to apply what is called DTM. I believed it could have more valuable and safer outcomes for both the patient/client and practitioner. My approach would address the safety and effectiveness of the delivery of this modality. At first, this approach seemed simple; however, once my research began, I found that the concept of DTM held some rather misleading and loose interpretations. At best, the concept of DTM, as it is generally presented, is a vague term. In over seven years of presenting the seminar entitled DEEP TISSUE MASSAGE: SAFE AND EFFECTIVE TECHNIQUES FOR COMMON PROBLEM AREAS, I found no one disagreed with the proposition that this term is, at best, vague. There are two other concepts that seem to add to the confusion, as well. These are, that in order for deep tissue massage to be effective, two things needed to exist: it must be painful, and excess force must be applied. These concepts still seem to be the consensus of most patients/clients and many practitioners. It is my belief that because of these two concepts and the lack of understanding of fascia and energy, the vagueness and the misunderstanding of the modality called DTM continue to persist. Patients/clients leave their massage treatment bruised and in pain, and practitioners injure themselves, as well, in the process. This is why I present my approach to DTM: that has no pain attached to it, uses less effort/force, and is safe and effective for both patient/client and practitioner.

When I first started presenting my seminars on DTM in January 2008, I was restricted by the information available regarding the true meaning of DTM. However, as time progressed more information became available about the tissue called "fascia" and its importance as it relates to the body's functioning and its systems. As information became much more available, it became evident to me that by working both the fascia and the energy of the body together, we could now go deeper into the intended tissues of the body than we could if we worked the tissues separately and in a conventional manner. Hence the term Jin Mo Qi Gong. This simply means the body's fascia (Jin Mo) and energy (Qi) connecting and working with (Gong). Einstein's theories and life-long work implied that energy is at the root of all existence. Without energy, there is nothing. If we work with the energy of the body, we automatically affect the tissue that is manifested through the energetic process. In this book, we will examine, illustrate, explain, and demonstrate how this takes place. The more we understand the essence of fascia and its close relationship to the energetic process of the body, the more we will understand how the body heals and takes care of itself.

The energy that I refer to is the energy we are provided with at birth, most commonly called **The Life Force or Qi**. This energy flows through the body and the body systems by way of the meridians. There are 12 standard meridians that match up with the body's organ systems. They are yin and yang. This qi (energy) flows through the meridians in a similar way that the electrical impulses flow through the nervous system. The point is that if that flow is blocked or hampered in any way, we can have pain, discomfort, or malfunction, and herein lies the importance of why we need to better understand fascia and how it affects the functional efficiency of the entire body, and most importantly, how it affects the body's flow systems, namely, blood(circulatory), lymph(lymphatic), electrical(nervous) and energy(meridian).

The bottom line is this: each of us must take responsibility for our own health. An excellent way to accomplish this task is to learn about and better understand fascia and energy, how they are connected, and how they work together. By knowing, understanding, and connecting with our fascia and energy and understanding how these two concepts work together, we can enhance and optimize the body's healing process. As practitioners, we need not induce pain. We need only exert minimal effort in our application of DTM. Regarding the aggressive approach for DTM, fascia responds negatively, and energy certainly does not need it. If we review and adjust the techniques and principles of the early teachings of DTM and incorporate my current concept of JIN MO QI GONG, as presented in this book, we can look forward to an injury-free career and many happy patients/clients.

Val Nardo, M.Ed., Ph.D., *retired.*

Introduction

The time has come. I can no longer put off the task of completing this treatise on the Deep Tissue Massage application simply because I may not have all the information that I believe I need. As you read this book, new information regarding fascia, DTM, energy principles, and technique becomes available, and it will continue to do so. In fact, since I first became involved in the practice of massage therapy twenty-two years ago, I have been writing this book. All of the activities that I have been involved in during my seven-year tenure with Cross Country Education, such as research, massage practice, and teaching, have been setting the foundation for the theories, principles, and applications that we will explore in this book. As I said, I will never have all of the information I need to write this book. I need to go with what I have now and hope for the best.

It all started when I was attending massage school twenty-two years ago. A visiting teacher, who was an acupuncturist, introduced me to the concept of energy as a human force. Up until that time I had not thought about energy very much, if at all. However, since that time, I have read, researched, practiced, studied, and focused on the concept of energy, searching for the relevance that energy has to our existence. After all of the research, study, teaching, and practice, all of which I continued to engage in, even after retirement, I have concluded that it comes down to Albert Einstein's scientific implications regarding energy: that is, **energy is the essence of everything.** It is with this underlying principle that I function and proceed.

As time passed, I gained more experience and knowledge about concepts that I had not thought about earlier. Einstein's energy implications began to take on new meaning and relevance to the practice of massage for me. I also became more aware of the tissue called fascia and began to look at it in a new light. My research helped me to understand that energy and fascia are closely related to one another and assist each other in their functions. So, after having assembled and taught the CEU program for Cross Country Education, I realize that I can no longer hold this valuable information for a better time. Now is the better time. Also, this information does not belong to me for safe keeping. It must be shared. I must release it with gratitude.

My seven-plus years of teaching CEU programs to healthcare professionals have provided me with many incredible learning moments. It has kept me in a continuous research mode so that I can keep up with new and exciting pieces of amazing data. What is most exciting is that the new and amazing data helps to validate the principles, concepts, and practices that I had been promoting from the beginning of the project, and it continued to do so. One last thought is that what I have learned through my experience in research, teaching, and practice in massage techniques and principles only scratches the surface of what is to come. There is so much more coming, and I am starting to see this in the content and attitude projected in current related literature. This brings me back to my task at hand: sharing my thoughts, beliefs, findings, and experiences through my book. Again, I share this information with gratitude. It is good to have company on this journey.

Chapter One:
In the Beginning: A Historical Perspective

Massage is the manipulation of soft tissue, which includes muscle and the vascular systems of nerves, lymph, and blood. We must never forget that all of this tissue is systematically surrounded by the grandest tissue of all, the mother of the body, fascia. It is my belief that this is where our treatment must begin, at least from a physical perspective, in order to obtain the most effective and safest results for our patients/clients and ourselves. Although I did not realize it early on, the concept "JIN MO QI GONG" was beginning to conceptualize in January 2008, when I began presenting massage therapy continuing education training for a company called Cross Country Education. The title of the program was DEEP TISSUE MASSAGE: SAFE AND EFFECTIVE TECHNIQUES FOR COMMON PROBLEM AREAS. In January 2008, I was in the early stages of reading about, studying, and practicing the principles of Qi Gong. Prior to that, my involvement with the concept of energy, or more accurately, human energy, was only on a general basis. An example of some of the writings that influenced me the most includes works such as "The Field" and "The Intention Experiment" by Lynne McTaggart; "Energy Medicine" by Donna Eden; "Quantum Healing" by Deepak Chopra, MD; "Molecules of Emotion," by Candace B. Pert, Ph.D.; "Vibrational Medicine," by Richard Gerber, MD.; "The Biology of Belief," by Bruce H. Lipton, Ph.D.; "The Relaxation Response," by Herbert Benson, MD.; "The Wellness Book," by Herbert Benson, MD and Eileen M. Stuart, R.N.; "Natural Health, Natural Medicine" and "Spontaneous Healing," by Andrew Weil MD.; "The Universe in a Single Atom," by His Holiness The Dalai Lama; "A Complete Guide to Chi-Gung," by Daniel Reid; "The Way of the Explorer," by Dr. Edgar Mitchell and "Cell Talk," by John E. Upledger, D.O., OMM, and as I said, this is just an example. There is so much more wonderful information available, simply for the taking.

In January 2008, I did not understand the value of energy, fascia, and massage therapy as possible collaborative concepts. I knew energy existed and was an important factor in the healing process. I knew about the meridians, chakras, qi, prana, and acupoints. I had an idea of the concept of fascia and its functions. However, I just had not yet put all of this information together in a way that would incorporate all of these ideas that produced safe and effective results. In retrospect, my thought process was disjointed. I had enough information empirically and from research to provide a valid, viable, and valuable training presentation, but as the program presentations continued, I realized that this idea was only in its infancy. At the time of this writing and since January 2008, I have traveled nationally in excess of 275,000 miles and presented nearly 300 seminars in approximately 44 states over a period of seven years. During this period of time the DTM program did evolve significantly. Now, the concept of "JIN MO QI GONG" has a fuller and richer meaning, a valid foundation, and a more vibrant life of its own. Also, since 2008, I have increased my knowledge of human energy, qi gong, working with the core, fascia, and the importance of their relationship. When I first began to develop the concepts of the DTM manual, something told me, you know, that little voice, that I must include fascia in the equation. Little did I know just how important the factor of fascia would be relative to what I was presenting in my DTM discussion. My program had been in an evolutionary state for nearly eight years, and it did not seem that it would ever stop evolving.

In the beginning, my presentations were rather sketchy, to say the least. One of the problems that I encountered was a lack of a sense of validity for the many ideas that surrounded the basic concept for safe and effective application of Deep Tissue Massage. There was a lot of good information; however, it did not support my approach regarding safety and effectiveness, which requires a non-aggressive application. The concept of fascia, as discussed in the literature, was dealt with separately and not necessarily as an integral part of the overall process. Energy was not even in the equation. However, I knew that what I was doing was working. It was working in my own private practice and positive results were being observed on a regular basis in the CEU program presentations. Early in January 2008, I made a request to the Universe to provide me with some form of validation to let me know that, at least, I was on the right track. I waited. Approximately seven months into the program presentations, I received my first sign of strong validation. An article appeared in the mid-summer edition of Massage Magazine. The author was Sean Riehl, a noted author, teacher, presenter of massage therapy techniques, and a contributing editor of Massage Magazine. That article was the initial answer to my validation request of the Universe. In this article, Mr. Riehl answers a question regarding the application of DTM. The question went something like this: "How can I keep from injuring my hands and fatiguing my fingers when I do deep tissue massage?" The person asking the question also stated, "I've heard deep tissue massage places a lot of stress on the therapist's body because of the strength required." This seems to continue to be a common belief regarding DTM. Mr. Riehl's answer provided me with the validation I most needed at that time. I had been familiar with Riehl's work since my initial massage training; however, I was not familiar with this particular philosophical approach to DTM, as presented in his article. Mr. Riehl's explanation of DTM was summarized with four words and these four words epitomized what I had been presenting for nearly seven months in my DTM program. Can you imagine how elated I was after discovering this information? This is what Riehl said about DTM. "The essence of DTM is not pain, and it is not effort. It is Ease, Patience, Sensitivity, and Presence." I now had some descriptive words to go with the applications for safe and effective DTM that I had been presenting. Riehl provided the "what to do," and I provided the "how to do it." We will get to the specifics later. Another key factor of importance that was still not quite formalized was why this process works. This began to take shape around the middle of 2009 after I discovered an organization that had been in existence since 2007. The organization is called The International Fascia Research Congress.

It is comprised of many practitioners and scientists from around the world who, up until 2007, had been working with fascia only on an individual level. They had now joined forces. It is my understanding that the major goal of the organization was to find out all there is to know about fascia and its relevance to the functions of the human body and its healing processes. The information developed and published by this organization has provided me with validation regarding fascia, fascia's relationship to energy and why massage therapy needs to take a good close look at fascia as the primary tissue when considering treatment options. In massage school, we did not spend a lot of time on fascia. In relationship to other systems in the body the time spent was insignificant. Over the last few years, I have heard from the seminar participants that fascia is being studied more in the basic massage training programs and that it is now considered one of the focal points for treatment options.

The Sean Riehl validation immediately provided meaning to an idea that I was attempting to promote, making a significant change in direction for the DTM program. In my first seminar presentations I began with an idea that I thought to be a meaningful ice-breaker. I presented an idea to the attendees that I hoped would help them with the learning process. It is not easy to sit in class for 6 hours and not have the mind wander. The concept is a simple one that I had been reading about and attempting to practice, as well.

I offered the idea of working with the concept of <u>mindfulness</u>. Initially, I did not make any real connection with massage in any form, let alone DTM. I was just sharing an idea to get my audience's attention. After reading Riehl's statement, I realized that this idea of mindfulness, though I was unaware when I initially used the word, was the very foundation for the entire process. Riehl's last word in his explanation of his philosophy of DTM is <u>Presence</u>, or, put another way, Mindfulness. I was already there and did not know it, but I know it now. Once I realized the importance of Riehl's implications regarding presence, I knew why I chose the mindfulness idea to open my class. It had just seemed like a good idea at the time. Again, my mind was blown away. How could this happen? Be careful what you request of the Universe. It will come to you in some way eventually when the time is right. What about the other three words: Ease, Patience, and Sensitivity? They did the same thing; they stated what DTM should look like, and if performed in this manner, it will promote a safe and effective massage with no pain and little effort. With these four words, Riehl independently identified and summarized the four major applications of my DTM program. My program has now evolved into a series of incorporated techniques. Ease, Patience, Sensitivity, and Presence implied that DTM need not be painful and with a reasonable amount of effort applied, would be safe and effective.

Two terms, pain and effort, seem to be the most common ones to surface when DTM is discussed by the patient/client and practitioner. Many continue to believe the saying "no pain, no gain." If a lot of effort is applied, and it is applied improperly, the practitioner opens the risk of injury to both the patient/client and self. It does not fit the maxim of "do no harm." Also, I could never understand what the logic is of creating pain to get rid of pain.

The chart below takes a closer look at the Presence or Mindfulness factor as it relates to DTM or any modality for that matter. Mindfulness helps us with awareness and consciousness. Being in a mindful state gives us the ability to focus on the task at hand (no pun intended). Being in a mindful state eliminates multitasking and greatly reduces our exposure to stress. Being in a mindful state promotes the achievement of optimal results. I use the following chart to show the progression of mindfulness as it relates to DTM and as it delivers a safe and effective service:

MINDFULNESS
INTENT
ENERGY

Ease, work the tissue slowly, with very little pressure, and increase as needed. Patience, as you work with the energy, wait for it to follow its intended path. Sensitivity, feeling and being aware of the flow of the energy so you can make needed adjustments. All are guided by the skillful tool of mindfulness.

It is important to start the process in the right frame of mind in order to ensure optimal results. As I stated earlier, we really do need to be <u>with</u> the patient/client on all levels. Being in a mindful state helps us to accomplish this and sets the tone for what is to come. I call this being <u>one</u> with the patient/client. We can not be concerned about what we will have for lunch today, what happened in traffic on the way to work, the tiff we had with our mate. We most likely have heard the term expressed as <u>being in the moment</u>. Being present with what we are doing. It is also called awareness. In this state, our senses become more alive and we can now follow more effectively the path of the mindfulness chart. Being in a mindful state will strengthen our intent, and our intent will drive our energy. It enhances and confirms our energy connection. Why is this important? The intent drives and guides the energy in and out, around and through our being. This means, of course, our muscles, tendons, blood, nerves, and lymph. It is this element of the chart that I believe is the essence of the safe and effective results for DTM. As Einstein implied, energy is all that is, meaning that everything we are, experience, taste, smell, feel, see, and hear is a manifestation of energy. We come from and <u>are</u> energy, a bundle of atoms. Our very essence is energy. As massage therapists, in order to manipulate the physical, we must first connect and work with the energy source. Energy needs very little, if any, effort to affect it or to guide its path, and it must move in order to be vital. The greater our level of mindfulness, the greater the potential for healing the mind, body, and spirit.

In summary, from a historical perspective, Sean Riehl provided a statement that clarified the concept of mindfulness as it relates to DTM. With his well-chosen words, Ease, Patience, Sensitivity, and Presence, he epitomized these collective applications being presented in my DTM program. For me and the DTM program, he provided a sense of validation. The concept of intent now took on new meaning, as well as, helping the energy to find its true path and its healing destination. As well, I now realize that energy is not only a vital part of the process but is the very essence and foundation of what transpires in the mind, body, and spirit. In Riehl's terms, when we work with Ease, Patience, Sensitivity, and Presence, we do not inflict pain, and we exert a reasonable amount of force, all the while working slowly and deliberately, waiting for the energy to do its work, being aware of what is transpiring energetically and physically and most importantly, making certain that you are in the moment, one with the patient/client.

Chapter Two:
Where Did I Come From and
Where Am I Going?

It's All About Energy

A question that keeps coming up in the DTM program is, can we consider DTM to be an energy technique? My answer is simple: why not? As humans, we have a tendency to separate most life features. For example, we have boundaries and borders, states, counties, countries, continents, nationalities, and political parties. We also have major disagreements and wars. In the practice of massage, we have physical techniques (Neuromuscular, Rolfing, Deep Tissue Massage, Trigger Point) and energy techniques (Reiki, Polarity Therapy, Sound Therapy) that we generally, do not work together. In science, we have the Universe. We have something called outer space. Personally, I do not promote the idea of outer space. I do not believe that it exists. It is all relative. It depends on where you are coming from. Recently, a picture was taken by one of NASA's high-powered telescopes of the Earth from the area of Saturn. In that picture Earth looks similar to what Saturn looks like from Earth. We are all part of the big picture. We are all connected. I feel that through a better understanding of the wonder of energy and the cosmos, we will be able to soften this separation complex that we humans seem to cling to with dear life and hopefully open up new channels of life experience. So, it seems logical to start with the concept of energy since everything is and comes from energy. Most folks, when we consider energy, think about gasoline, the fuel for our cars, electricity to heat our homes, run our appliances, or light our rooms. However, within the last fifteen to twenty years the term "human energy" has become more prominent as another type of energy that relates to the functioning of the human being. In Western society, this concept is relatively new, at least from an acceptance point of view. Of course, as mentioned earlier, Einstein ushered in the quantum concept that suggests that everything is connected and that we <u>are</u> energy and energy drives everything. We are the Universe. In Traditional Chinese Medicine, which, according to some historians, could be as old in some form as 10,000 years, energy and energy principles have been explored and practiced on some level. Today, these principles and practices are being studied and validated as legitimate medical processes. Some of these practices are acupuncture, acupressure, meditation, qi gong, tai chi, herbology, polarity therapy, reiki, craniosacral therapy, and many others. These concepts have little or no side effects. The downside is that one must be committed and have patience and trust regarding the treatment for it to be effective. Unfortunately, Western society lacks these three traits and consequently has resorted to and become addicted to the quick fixes of drugs and surgery. However, biologically, naturally, and realistically, the only way healing can take place is through the body's own abilities and efforts.

In relationship to massage therapy, it seems logical that we incorporate energy principle and energy technique into the treatment process rather than consider them as a separate entity. Sometimes, just thinking about or being aware of the energy and its relationship to human function is all one needs to be effective in the massage treatment process. The sooner we realize that we are in this together and everything is connected, the more effective and optimal our results will be. **We are all in this together, and everything is connected**. The cosmos is energy, and we are energy. Understanding and incorporating this concept into our thought process will enhance and increase, from a massage perspective, the body's healing powers and our involvement in the treatment process. Energy is the foundation and the essence of life. In Chinese medicine, it is called "life force." Incorporating energy techniques into any massage routine will enhance the process on many levels: physical, psychological, spiritual, and, of course, energetic. Also, the body's healing mechanism is provided with basic and natural tools that it needs to function at the highest level of performance. Traditional

Chinese Medicine has operated on this premise for thousands of years with great success. We need to pay attention to this piece of information. Because of energy, everything contains the same elements and principles of existence. For example, the atom, of which we have "kazillions," mirrors the structures and movement of the cosmos. The cell mirrors the structure and function of the body. We are made of the same elements as the cosmos; we are stardust. Fascia has similar functions as dark matter in the Universe, holding everything together. As mentioned earlier, depending on where you view the Universe, everything has a similar look. Everything is relative in the Universe. In order for us to maintain life we all have to breathe the same air. We are in the Universe, the Universe is in us, and we are the Universe. The concept of separation regarding the physical and the energetic is simply impractical, and when one follows the separation principle in relationship to medical treatment, it is inefficient and ineffective.

In summary, the questions "Where did I come from?" and "Where am I going?" are relatively simple to answer. I come from Stardust, and my destination goal is to return to the stuff of the stars, my original home. I am energy, and energy is all there is. Your existence in the human realm should also be an easy concept to accept. Once you understand human energy, it makes a lot of sense. TCM has understood and practiced the connection of energy and physical principles of life force for thousands of years with monumental success, and today, many of these ancient principles and practices are being proven to be valid and effective medically from a scientific level. My goal in this chapter has been to provide information that will convince and encourage you to pursue further, on your own, the importance of energy and how, if used properly can positively affect the results of physical treatment when incorporated with energy treatment protocols. As mentioned earlier, we start with mindfulness, which strengthens our intention and increases our connection with energy, where everything begins and ends. Energy is the prime mover of all. With a strong intention, which can be nothing more than a thought process, which is the strongest form of energy we have at our disposal, we can move mountains. Today, there are many energy processes utilized in allopathic medicine, including x-ray, laser, ultrasound, EKG, PET Scan, MRI, EEG, ECG, CAT Scan, Radiography, and Tomography, as examples. Of course, these protocols are not generally considered to be energy medicine in the same way that, let's say, Polarity Therapy, Reiki, or Craniosacral Therapy are considered energy medicine in the alternative or integrative medicine realm. They are extremely effective and, for the most part, very safe. Let us be honest: allopathic medicine would be archaic without the energy practices mentioned above. However, I believe we are almost there, folks. My hope is that, eventually, Integrative Medicine will be a reality when ancient, present-day and future medical methods will join forces and benefit all mankind, as it well should.

I want to leave you with one more energy thought. What is the approximate number of <u>atoms</u> in the human body? The average person is around 150 lbs. The formula for working the problem out is 7 x (10 to the power of 27). The answer is 70,000,000,000,000,000,000,000,000,000 (octillion). Have fun with that one. Thirty to a hundred trillion <u>cells</u> in the human body seems hard to wrap around the mind, as well, but the potential energetic force is even more mind-bending. We need to be utilizing this energy to help the human healing process.

Chapter Three:
The Mother of The Body

What can be said about fascia? The answer is, finally, plenty. When I developed my original DTM program in 2007, I knew there was more to massage than muscle, tendon, and ligament. Yes, there is; it's FASCIA. The problem was that not much had been studied or written about it in the available medical literature. In massage school, it was talked about as part of the connective tissue system with very little exploration or explanation, just as it has been treated for 500 years of medical development. It has been grossly ignored. Without my knowing, at the same time I was developing and presenting my program, an organization dedicated to the study of fascia had come into existence called the International Fascia Research Congress. Also, I stumbled onto a piece of information that specifically states how fascia and DTM need to be treated for the most optimal results. Sean Riehl simply stated that DTM needs to be approached in four ways: EASE, PATIENCE, SENSITIVITY, PRESENCE. This approach is critical because of fascia, not muscle.

We will discuss all of this shortly. With this new information my program took on new life and energy. This program's concepts are very simple as they relate to DTM and fascia, and I would challenge anyone qualified to prove it with the scientific method.

Let's get started. What is fascia? Fascia is connective tissue. Where is it in the body? Quite simply, it is everywhere, and I mean everywhere. It wraps around everything in the body: muscles, blood vessels, lungs, and even cells. It is the most prevalent tissue in the body. You get the idea. With the new research being conducted, fascia is being found to have many functions. Regarding massage/DTM and fascia's role, its two most important functions are support/structure and body protection. Support/structure holds us together and gives us shape.

Without this, we would be an amoeba-like creature. Protection is a little more complicated. As I stated earlier, fascia is wrapped around everything in the body, and this wrapping is one continuous piece of material with no seams. So when something is happening in your lower back, but you feel it in your shoulder, this is sometimes called referred pain, back to protection. So, if the fascia is wrapped around everything, including circulatory, lymphatic, nervous, and meridian systems, we get food and oxygen through the circulatory system, our lymphatic system helps eliminate our toxins, our nervous system keeps us moving, etc., our meridian system keeps yin and yang energy in balance or in homeostasis. When these systems are free to flow, we are more apt to be healthy, and when they are blocked, we are more at risk of physical and bodily malfunction.

What state does fascia go into when in the protection mode? It constricts in the protection mode. What can cause the fascia to constrict in the protective mode? Some of the things that can cause this constriction in fascia are accidents, such as auto, fall, scare, and stress, just to mention a few. So, when in the constrictive mode, the blood, lymph, nervous, and energy systems have impaired flow and can cause pain, numbness, HBP, soreness, and toxicity, again, just to mention a few. It is similar to the mother/infant situation when they are confronted with a dangerous event. The mother will instantly hold the infant tighter and not let go, at all costs, until it is safe. The fascia responds the same way and, in doing so, can cause pain and discomfort in the area it is protecting and possibly other areas. This is why I call fascia the mother of the body.

Let us wrap this up by stating some interesting facts about fascia. Fascia is known as the communications grid for the body. It is the way the body talks to itself. There are ten times more nerve sensations in fascia tissue than in muscle tissue. There is more fascia in the body than any other tissue (similar to dark matter in the Universe). There is more dark matter in the Universe than any other material. It has been considered the glue of the cosmos. It keeps things where they need to be. Fascia keeps things where they need to be in the body. The water content of the fascia is sixty percent, and forty percent is other material, such as elastin and collagen or ground material, which makes it imperative to drink adequate amounts of water to maintain a healthy fascia state. As mentioned previously, fascia has ten times more nerve sensitivity than muscle. This leads me to the statement that **fascia knows**. It can sense before something happens that it is going to happen, giving it time to go into the protective mode early. This is an example of how the energy field and fascia work together. Another example is the fascia and the meridian system working together as they work closely with the circulatory system, lymphatic system, and nervous system, helping to keep the flow systems functioning properly. One last fascia tidbit: it has the capability of pushing against and withstanding pressure of 2,000 lbs. psi before breaking down. Who wins this battle?

Chapter Four:
Our Energy Source

Where does our energy to move really come from?

It is called many things: Dan Tien, Hara, Root Chakra, Kundalini, and Fire in the Belly. If you are a physical therapist or an exercise specialist, you would most likely call it the **core**. Think about it for a moment: every move we make, from smallest to largest, comes from the core. So, where is the core? It is the area just below the belly button. If we are not using our core to perform our daily physical activities, we will move robotically, which places stress on our tendons and ligaments, causing soreness, fatigue, and possibly pain. Performing massage in this manner may cause a feeling of tension. This can shorten the time we will be able to perform physical movement comfortably and it can place us at risk for injury to our patient/client and self.

Working with the core helps us get what I call soft hands, which promotes sensitivity. More on this later. Working with the core also relates directly to the standard phrase "proper body mechanics." One of the most effective ways that I have been able to achieve the state of proper body mechanics is through an ancient Chinese exercise called Qi Gong. Simply stated, this exercise incorporates breath work, mild and slow movement and intention. The term literally means "working with the energy." By practicing Qi Gong or even mild forms of Tai Chi, one can develop a relaxed, fluid, safe, and effective movement style for massage therapy application.

Chapter Five:
The What and How of Deep Tissue Massage

In order to address this issue properly and in detail we need to go back to the beginning. As I said, when I started this project I did not have a good understanding of the concepts involved, and, what I thought I knew was based mostly on personal and perceptional experience. This is not a good knowledge foundation. In my defense there was not very much reliable information available regarding deep tissue massage and what was available was vague. This is all discussed earlier in the book. The point being, I ended up in an entirely different place seven years later. No matter what you call it, or what you perceive you are doing, and how you do what you are doing, the application must have connection and validity. When I started the deep tissue massage project, that did not exist. I developed some "how to" techniques for common muscle conditions and injuries but something was missing – there had to be more. I kept searching for the answer. About six or seven months into the program I came across an article in Massage Magazine written by Sean Riehl simply answering a question about how to approach deep tissue massage so as not to injure oneself. The implication of the question was that when working too hard there is a risk of hurting oneself. After reading Riehl's simple statement I realized I was already doing what he proposed, I just did not have labels for it. Riehl defined what DTM is and how it might be perceived. I began to realize that there were many moving parts to this process. I will now present the moving parts. I have already touched on these concepts but let us discuss them as they fit into the context of how we perform JIN MO QI GONG. Also, we will talk about why this process works and seems to make sense.

Let us take a closer look at those moving parts. The list includes fascia, energy, Mr.Riehl's premise regarding DTM, the core and maintaining an attitude of safety of both patient/client and you as the practitioner.

We will start with the DTM premise of Riehl, "Deep tissue massage is not pain and it is not effort. It is ease, patience, sensitivity and presence." This statement represents a simple, safe and effective approach to DTM. What I was presenting in my DTM course fit right into this premise. What I discovered was that if you approach muscle, tendon, ligament and flow systems, by focusing on fascia first, you will be able to effect these tissues faster, more effectively and more efficiently. One of the key factors about fascia that makes my DTM technique work is: fascia does not like to be treated aggressively. In fact the more aggressively the approach the tighter the constriction. The first word ease presents the manner in which you enter the fascia tissue. You enter the tissue with ease, lightly and slowly, feeling the tissue giving under your hands as if melting. As the tissue melts, you are let in deeper, which satisfies the notion of DTM. It will be amazing how deep one can go utilizing this approach, which is not painful and requires very little effort. As the tissue melts, the organs, such as, blood and lymph, nerves and energy, will begin to open up and flow more freely, providing oxygen and food to the muscles, and detoxing the body. There will be greater mobility, less pain and heightened sensation, which in turn, provide healing in the muscles. Ease is a safe and effective DTM tool for client/patient and therapist.

The next word in the process is patience. This simply means waiting for the changes to take place in the energy flow and in the tissue, initially fascia, and eventually muscle. Working slowly can also be helpful in detecting possible issues. Waiting with care is key regarding patience.

The third Riehl factor is sensitivity. What is it and how we achieve it? From a physical perspective this is a key factor. In massage we manifest our sensitivity, primarily, by the way we use our hands. So, if we are generating the power to perform the massage activity from our hands they will become tight and fatigued very quickly and begin to feel sore or even painful. When we work this way we have, what I call, hard hands and hard hands inhibit sensitivity. This will also put us at risk for injury to the patient/client and ourselves. The energy must come from the core. It is that simple. An ideal way to achieve this feeling of connection between the physical and the energetic is by practicing an ancient exercise form called Qi Gong. I will discuss Qi Gong in more detail later.

The fourth word that Riehl uses to describe DTM is <u>presence</u>. By placing it last I believe he draws attention to the word. He is saying let us start here. In fact, I unwittingly, from the very beginning, did present this idea in my classes, and continued to do so subsequently, simply because the whole process needs to start with this concept. The only difference is that Riehl called it <u>presence</u> and I call it <u>mindfulness</u>. Being <u>mindful</u> helps us to be aware of what is now happening in our patient's/client's being and in our being, as well. Being in this state, as much as possible, helps us to make changes quickly, which can prevent injury to the patient/client and practitioner and as it helps us to be aware of changes, we can respond accordingly. Being mindful is critical in terms of being able to deal with the patient/client on all of the levels that may present themselves during treatment, such as: physical, emotional, mental, spiritual and energetic. We owe it to our patient/client to be with them in the most optimal way possible. After all, the manner in which the massage therapist presents herself/himself cannot be handled (no pun intended) as just a job. I believe that massage therapy is a noble calling and should be approached as such.

Chapter Six:
An Ancient Gift

Qi Gong is an ancient Chinese exercise form. The practice of Qi Gong has a history in the Chinese tradition of 4,000 to 6,000 years, and some historians have speculated as far in the past as 10,000 years. Qi Gong is based on the principle of Yin and Yang, which are opposite forces that exist in the universe, in the environment, and in the human body. The most common opposite combination is positive and negative. However, we should not look at these opposing forces as good and bad. We must view these opposites as forces that must exist together in balance in order for energy to exist, and as implied by Einstein, energy is all there is. We are energy, the trees are energy, the mountains are energy, etc. Qi Gong is a very efficient and effective exercise method for connecting and working with the various energy fields around and in us. It is time-tested and time-proven as a valid health practice in both self-care and therapeutic procedures. There are two energy formulas that are important in the Qi Gong process: The Three Treasures and The Three Powers. The Three Treasures are Jing, essence; Qi, energy; and Shen, soul or spirit. The essence is the core or the root of life. The Qi is the "life force" that runs around and through the body. The Qi is also manifested in the breath. The Shen is the soul, and the mind is the spirit of our being. It is enriched by the Qi of the body. The Three Powers or the sources of energy are Heaven, Earth, and Humanity or the universe, the environment, and humans. The Chinese believe that in order to be healthy and remain healthy the Jing or original energy must be protected and maintained. Qi Gong is an ideal way to help this take place.

With Qi Gong, we work with The Three Powers to provide a balanced flow of energy from the universe, the environment, and ourselves. The Shen (spirit) is the governing treasure that keeps all three treasures in balance. As we practice the art of Qi Gong, keep in mind that we will be attempting to relate the physical movement and the energy movement to the application of massage and other bodywork activity. In doing this, we will hopefully develop a better sense of awareness of body and mind, a better sense of core, and a better sense of balance, as well as the synchronicity between the body and hands. Finally, the foundation of Qi Gong is based on three factors: intent, movement, and proper breathing. We have already talked about intent; however, to remind you, <u>focus</u> is key. Have a goal. Qi Gong is not a judgmental activity. Do the best you can with good intentions. Know what you want to accomplish. Movement can be looked at in two ways: physical and energetic. You can perform Qi Gong with the movement of one of its many beautiful forms or you can perform it while perfectly still. The key to energetic movement is that it can be done with intent, requiring little physical ability. Lastly, we have proper breathing. Simple, just breathe deeply, slowly, and naturally. The main concept to keep in mind is that you intend energy to places it needs to go to and from. Do not try to make it happen. Do not force it. Enjoy and feel the energy as it makes its journey. *This chapter is accompanied by two sets of illustrations: a Qi Gong warm-up exercise and a Qi Gong - Tai Chi form called The Four Winds. This will help you to learn movement from the core which will save your hands. Enjoy!*

Qi Gong Warm-Up

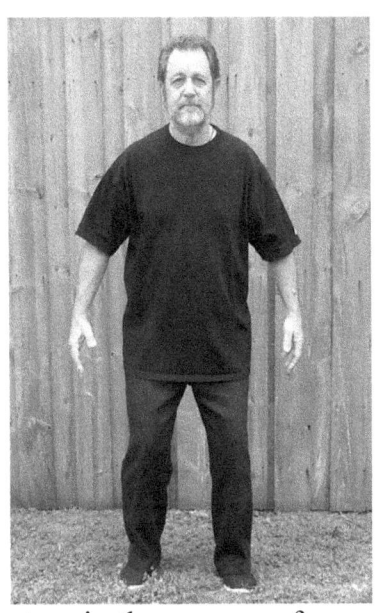

Start each posture in the warm-up form with the power stance. Arms and hands are hanging loosely to the sides of the body. The feet are positioned approximately shoulder-width apart. The knees are bent even with the toes. Form a slight smile to promote joy. Focus on something in front of you. Each posture in this form will end with the power stance. Become aware of your breathing pattern. The breathing rule is simply this: any movement away from the body, breathe in. With movement toward the body, you breathe out. Softly touch the roof of the mouth with the tongue. This connects the two meridians in the front and back of the body. These meridians are called the governing and the conceptual. These meridians are responsible for the circulation of Qi within the entire meridian system, as well as the body and its organs. This posture may stand alone while you connect with your energy and balance.

First, warm up posture – raising up to heaven and pushing down on earth.

Following the power stance, move slowly, palms down, lifting your arms and hands, towards heaven. Lift your arms and hands to about

 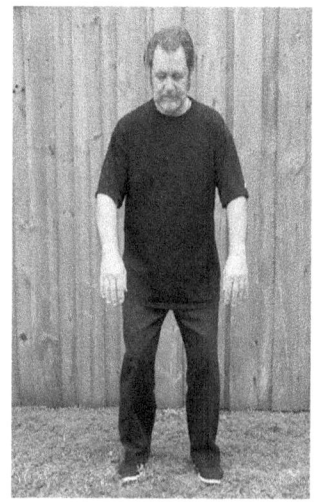

eye level, then lower your arms and hands to the original position. You can do this posture for 36 repetitions. The movement should be relaxed and fluid. The arms and hands should feel as though they are being lifted by the energy and not muscle and tendons. Breathing should be simple in as you go up and out as you come down. End this posture with the power stance. One rep is up and down.

Second Warm-Up posture - playing with the energy globe

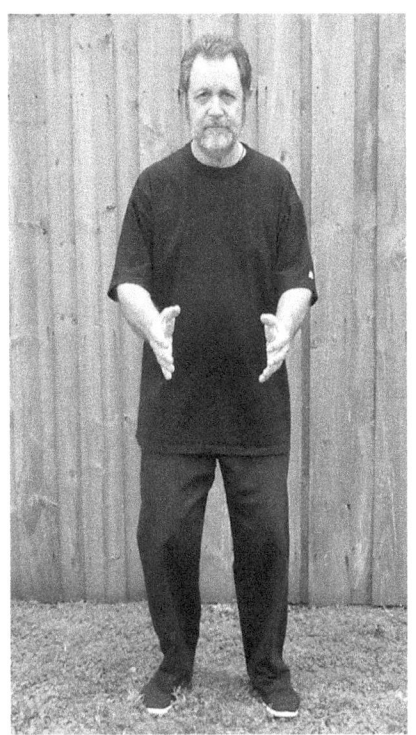 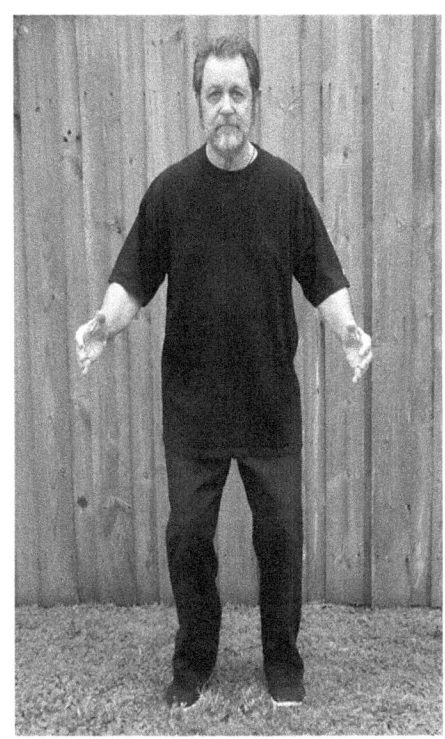

Start with the power stance. Playing with the energy globe is relatively simple. You bring your hands close together in front of you, not touching, and then spread them apart, imagining an energy globe in the middle. These two moves are basic. You may move the globe in several different directions, as well as if you were holding a real globe. Attempt to complete a series of reps consisting of approximately 36 in number. Again, end this posture with the power stance. Breathe out as you squeeze the globe and in as you expand the globe. One rep is in and out.

Third warm-up posture - twisting the trunk

Start with the power stance. Then, move into the prayer position over the head. Now twist to the left, back to the center, and then to the right and back to the center, repeat. A right and left move consists of one rep. Breathe in as you twist to the right or left, and breathe out as you twist back to the front position. Complete 36 reps and then end with the power stance.

Fourth warm-up posture - bending the trunk

Start with the power stance. Move into the prayer position over the head. Bend to the left, then back to the center, and then bend to the right. Breathe in as you bend right or left. Breathe out as you bend to the center position. Right and left bends consist of one rep. Complete 36 reps and then end with the power stance.

Fifth warm-up posture - offering gratitude

Start with the power stance. Then, move the arms out to the side of the body and up to the prayer position over the head. Then, move the hands down into a prayer position at the chest. Breathe in as you move upward, and breathe out as you move back to the center. Offer gratitude at this point. Do this posture as many times as you wish, depending on the number of things for which you are grateful.

Sixth warm-up posture – massaging the abdomen

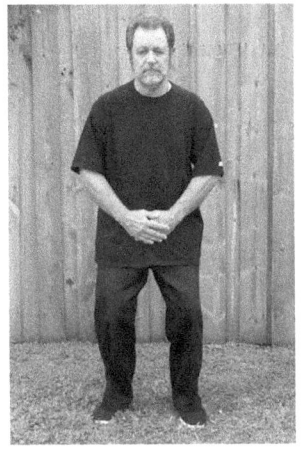

Start with the power stance posture. Move the arms and hands/palms into and around the abdomen with small circles. Make a complete circle covering the entire abdominal area, starting right to the left, ascending, transverse, and descending colon. Make 36 mini circles, 12 each section, and then reverse the process, starting left to right, descending, transverse, and ascending colons. End with the power stance posture.

Seventh warm-up posture - bowing to the universe

Start with the power stance posture. Move into a prayer stance at chest level and then bow. Bow to the universe and those who may be participating in this form with you. End this form with the power stance.

The Four Winds Form

This next section contains illustrations of a form called The Four Winds. This form consists of both Qi Gong and Tai Chi postures. This form will provide a sense of energy production, bringing the energy up through the body from the core into the arms and hands. At this point the arms and hands will be working through the energy produced rather than the action of muscle and tendon. This will help to get a sense of relaxation in the arms and hands. This will provide a better release for the energy produced so that the energy does the work and not the arms and hands. I consider this form to be a soft form of mixed Tai Chi and Qi Gong. This form, as in the warm-up form, will begin with the power stance; however, since we are incorporating Tai Chi and Qi Gong, we will not use the power stance again until we begin a direction change. This provides a flow between each posture, giving it a feel of a Tai Chi form with a Qi Gong intent.

First Four Winds posture - lifting arms and hands up to heaven and back to earth.

Begin this form facing East. The following postures will lead you to face North, West, South and finish facing East, hence the Four Winds.

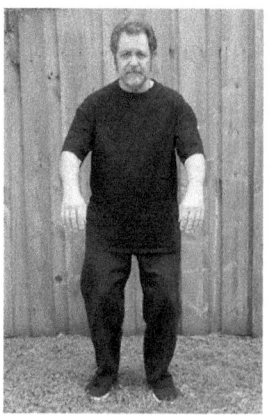 

Facing forward and knees bent slightly, raise the arms and hand toward the heavens, palms down.

 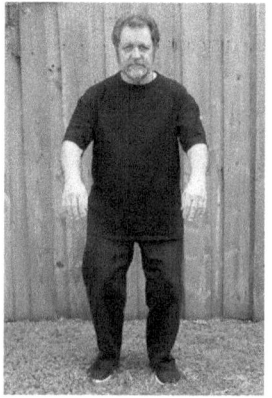

Raise your arms and hands to about chin level. Then, lower your arms back down to the original position, keeping the hands and arms supple and relaxed, free of any tension.

Up and down movement consists of one rep. Work toward completing 36 reps. When you complete this first posture, go into the next posture. Remember that in this form, each posture flows into the next with no power stance in between. The power stance is only used between direction changes, E, N, W, and S.

When you move outward, breathe in, and when you move inward, breathe out.

Second Four Winds posture – lunging to the right, up to heaven, then down to earth

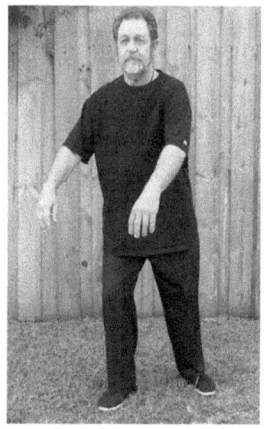  

While turning to the right 45°, raise your arms and hands, palms down, to heaven and then back to earth. As you raise to heaven, you will fill the right leg with energy moving forward, and as you come back to earth, you will fill the left leg with energy moving backward. This is a lunging move that is common in the practice of Tai Chi. You can repeat this posture 36 times. This will be a rocking movement. As above, follow the in-out breathing pattern.

Third Four Winds Posture – playing with the universal

Continue in the 45° to the right position and form an energy globe. In this position you are free to move the globe in any direction that you wish. You can compress and expand the globe at will, as well. Be aware of these moves, primarily from your core. This move should be smooth, slow and deliberate, as if dancing. There is really no need to count reps in this move. Do as many reps as you wish and when it feels good to stop you may go into the next posture.

Fourth Four Winds posture - raising arms and hands to heaven and back to earth

From the left, as you complete playing with the energy globe, move your left leg and foot to the left at about 90°. Now begin to raise your arms and hands, palms down, to heaven and back down to earth. Complete 36 reps. As you complete the 36 reps, bring your right foot and leg parallel to your left foot and leg. If you started out facing the East direction you will now be facing the North direction. Go to the power stance and repeat postures one through four in the North, West, and South directions. You will end up facing the East. Breathe in for moves outward and out for moves inward.

 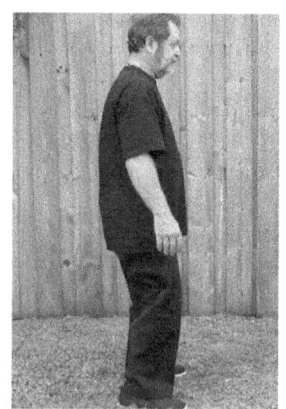

Chapter Seven:
Application Illustrations

This chapter has a set of illustrations of my JIN MO QI GONG technique. The body areas covered generally are the neck, shoulder, upper mid lower back, hip, thigh, and leg.

NECK	Longissimus
Sternocleidomastoid	Quadratus Lumborum
Scalenes	**HIP**
SHOULDER	Gluteus Minimus
Trapezius	Gluteus Medius
Levator Scapula	Gluteus Maximus
Rhomboids	Tensor Fascia Lata
Latissimus Dorsi	Iliotibial Band
Subscapularis	Piriformis
Supraspinatus	**THIGH**
Infraspinatus	Quadriceps
Teres Minor	Hamstrings
UPPER MID LOWER BACK	**LEG**
Rotators	Gastrocnemius
Multifidus	Soleus
Iliocostalis	Peroneals

Keep in mind, in JIN MO QI GONG, that even though we are attempting to affect the muscles listed above, we are focusing on the fascia as the primary tissue in our approach. The fascia is the master tissue that holds everything in place and is the protector of all other tissues in the body. My theory follows the principles of homeopathic medicine and craniosacral therapy. The basic homeopathic principle stated simply is that <u>less is best,</u> and craniosacral therapy is applied with the touch of about the weight of a nickel. The point is in order to affect the fascia, which controls that which it is wrapped around requires very little pressure. In fact, it reacts negatively to heavy or aggressive applications. It should also be noted that the applications in the JIN MO QI GONG process do not require strict usage. For example, you may apply the strokes of any one area alone, such as the neck, the lower back, or the leg, depending on the patient/client's needs. Conversely, you are also able to use the entire JIN MO QI GONG process, as shown here, as a complete massage service. This process was designed to be used as one of many tools for the massage therapist. For example, the ideal way to use the system is to combine it with other techniques, such as craniosacral therapy, Swedish massage, acupoint therapy, stretching, energy techniques, as well as, hydrotherapy. If your patient/client is having a lower back problem, you may want to consider using the lower back, hip, and thigh techniques in the JIN MO QI GONG process and other modalities of your choice. With that, let us take a look at the overall structure of the JIN MO QI GONG process. These illustrations are taken directly from the training manual that was utilized in the Cross Country Education CEU programs and the HomeCEUConnection video programs mentioned earlier. I apologize for the quality of the photos; however, you are viewing vintage material.

One last reminder, breathing follows the Qi Gong technique, outward move, breathe in, inward move, breathe out.

NECK

SHOULDER

UPPER BACK

MID BACK

LOW BACK

HIP

THIGH

LEG

NECK - STEPS 1 & 2

Step 1 is the basic position for the therapist to perform the neck applications in the Jin Mo Qi Gong therapy. The patient/client is supine. The therapist is seated at the head so that both arms can straddle the head and neck region comfortably. This view will give you an idea of what the first move will be. In this view a therapist is 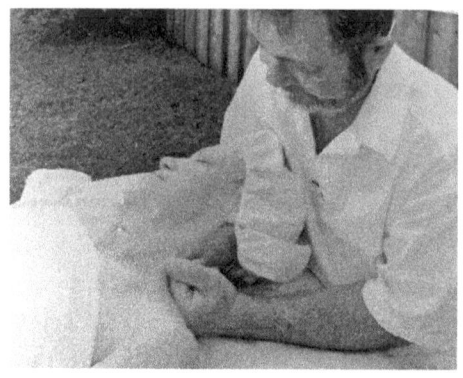 working the left side of the neck. Grasp the occipital area of the head in the palm of the right hand. This provides comfort for the patient/ client and maneuverability of the head so that the left neck is easily accessible. While cradling the occipital area of the head with the right hand, place the left hand with palm up and fingers extended distal to proximal of the neck, slowly and lightly rake down proximal to distal towards the shoulder. Proceed in this manner several times so as to detect where the problem areas that need attention may be. After you determine the needs of the patient/client in this area, you may begin with the picture shown in step 2 in the neck series. Again, you are not required to utilize all moves in any series. Choose any that work for you; just remember, ease, patience, sensitivity, and mindfulness. Work with a soft fist from the proximal to distal areas of the neck to loosen up the fascia. Do this several times before going into the next moves. Remember, all of the therapist's moves originate in the core. This is a closer view of move 2 in the neck area using the soft fist, lightly sliding along the scalenes, traps,

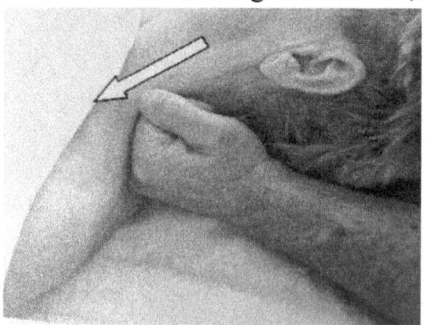 and levator scapula from the head to the shoulder area in the neck. Work slowly; use light pressure first, and add pressure as you proceed, staying within a tolerable comfort range.

NECK - STEPS 3, 4 & 5

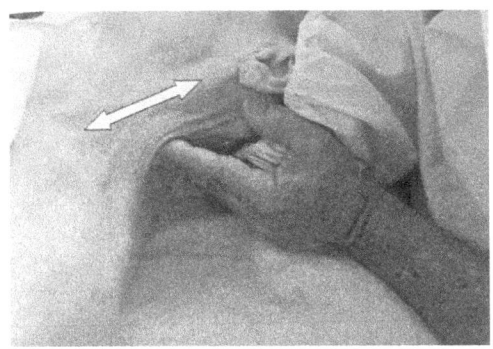

The next three steps can be completed utilizing 2 - 4 extended fingers, first sliding along the scalenes, traps, and levator scapula from head to shoulder joint and back. Start with light pressure and add pressure within a tolerable comfort range. Work slowly and mindfully. Do this several times as needed. The next move with the fingers will be in the same general area. However, you will focus more on the spot of concern. Again, working 2 - 4 extended fingers in cross-fiber friction in the area of concern. Do this several times as needed, working slowly and lightly. The next move, again using 2 - 4 extended fingers, will be circular friction in the area of concern. Do this several times, working slowly and lightly. Remember, all moves originate in the core.

NECK - STEP 6

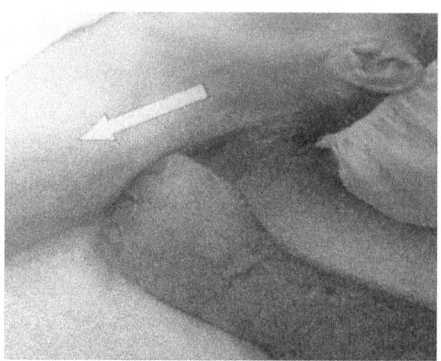

Working the trapezius and levator scapula muscles using the closed fist and supported thumb, slide in the direction from the head toward the shoulder joint. Place the other hand on the occiput and apply a slight stretch while performing the stroke. Remember, all moves originate in the core. Stay within a tolerable comfort range.

NECK - STEP 7

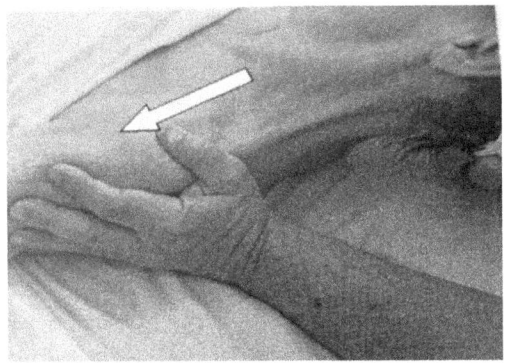

   With the palm of the hand, stretch the scalenes while placing the other hand on the occiput and apply a pull or stretch in the opposite direction. Work slowly and deliberately and remember, all moves originate in the core. Remember, work within a tolerable comfort range. Of course, both sides are worked is the same manner.

SHOULDER - STEP 1

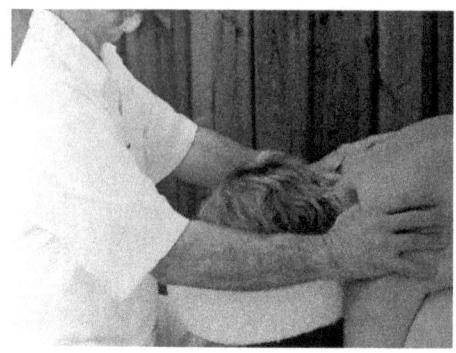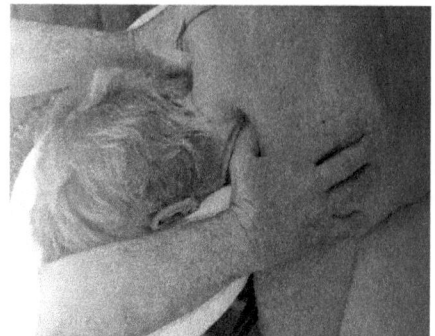

While in a seated position at the head, work the upper traps, medial to lateral. The technique of compression is applied with the thumb. Pressure is light at first, with mild increases as you progress and as needed. Work slowly and use the body and the core to apply force for the stroke. Do not apply pressure with the hands, arms, or thumbs. Work from the core.

SHOULDER - STEP 2

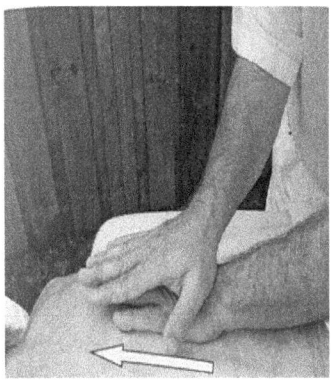

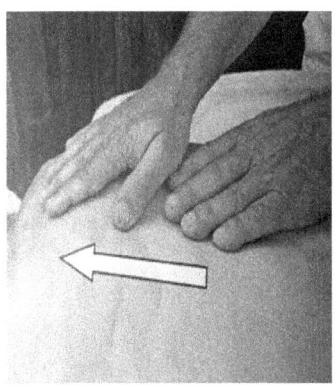

In the second move for the shoulder, we will focus on the latissimus dorsi and low and mid traps. The 2 hand positions shown above are hand behind hand and supported hand on hand. Use whichever one is comfortable or both. Begin the move as low as the sacral area and work your way up to the shoulder area. This will help to loosen fascia and release toxins. This move is a slide or glide similar to an effleurage stroke. Start with light pressure, increase as needed, but stay within a tolerable comfort range. Move slowly and use the body and core for the force of the stroke not the hand and arms.

SHOULDER - STEP 3

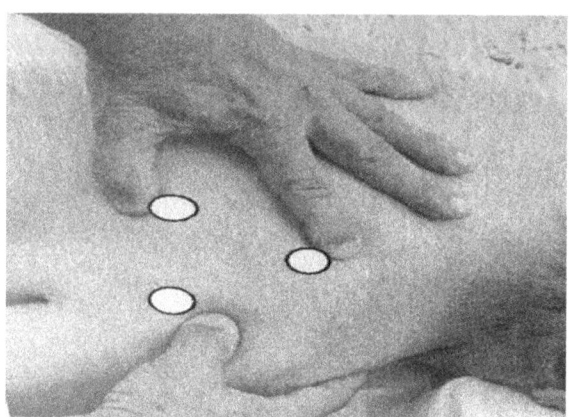

This view identifies the three areas on the scapula that may have trigger points and tenderness. Working these areas with a trigger point stroke or compression 3 x's, 15 – 20 secs each, will help to reduce the tenderness of the trigger points. The amount of pressure should be within the patient/client's comfort tolerance. You can also utilize a circular friction with the thumb on each area identified. Again, work within the comfort tolerance. Work slowly and deliberately utilizing the body and core to provide power for the stroke rather than the thumb, hand, or arm.

SHOULDER - STEP 4

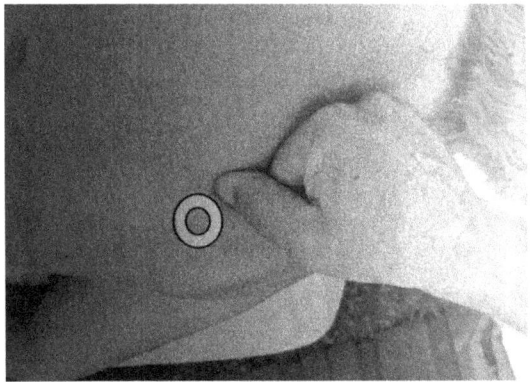

This move is a circular friction along the medial border of the scapula. As you can see, this is a supported thumb move. Start with light pressure and add pressure as needed or as appropriate. Work slowly and utilize the core and body for the force of the stroke, not the hand or thumb. Remember, work within a tolerable comfort range.

SHOULDER - STEP 5

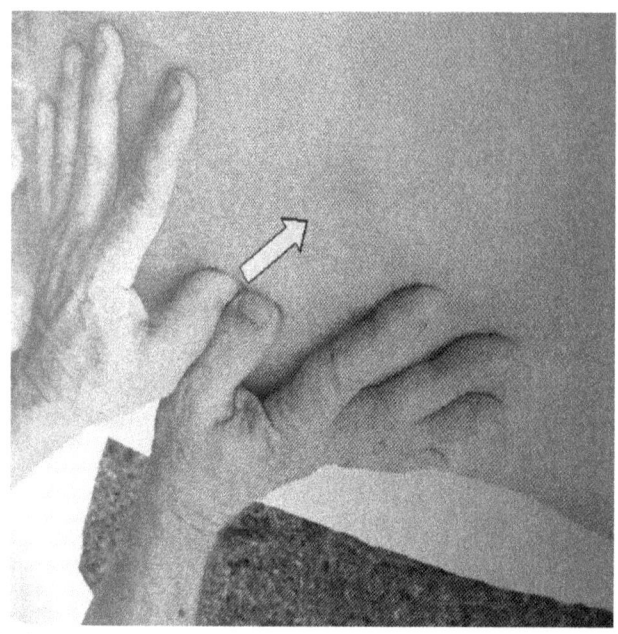

This is an illustration of slide and friction in the direction of the fibrosing lateral to medial on the infraspinatus. This is a supported thumb position. Use the weight of the body and the core to provide the source of energy for the stroke. Work slowly and deliberately, using light pressure at first and adding pressure as needed within a tolerable comfort range.

SHOULDER - STEP 6

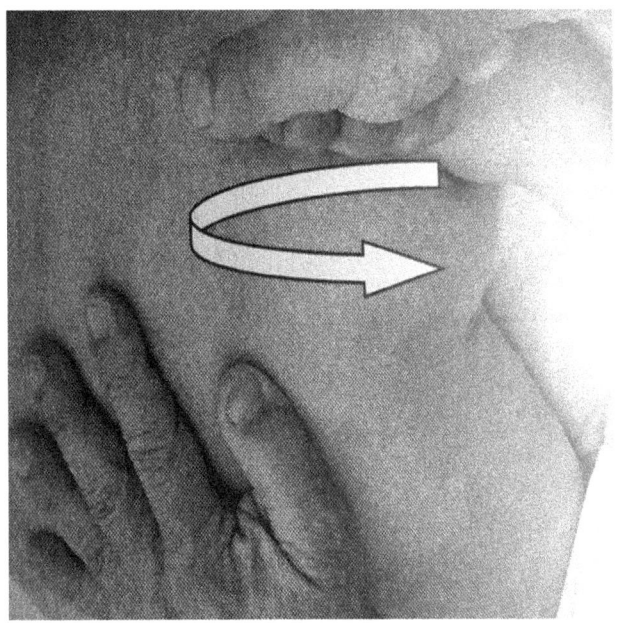

This move is an exaggerated circular friction with the fist around the surface of the infraspinatus. This move will also affect the subscapularis. Start with light pressure and add pressure as needed within a tolerable comfort range. Move slowly and deliberately, utilizing the body and the core to provide power for the stroke.

SHOULDER - STEP 7

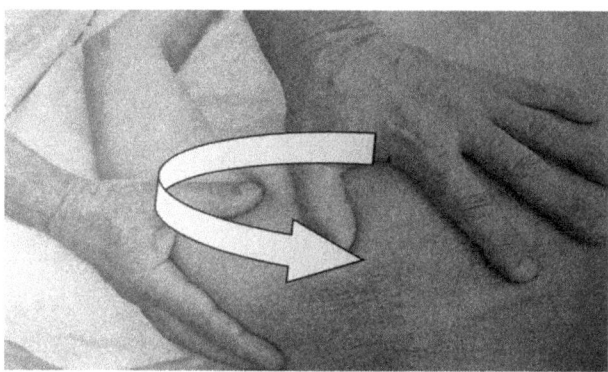

This move involves a stretch and circular friction affecting the scapula, infraspinatus, and subscapularis. Thumbs and palms of both hands are utilized. The hand at the joint is a stabilizer, and the other moves the muscles. Move slowly and deliberately, starting with light pressure and increasing the pressure as needed, always working within a tolerable comfort range. Use the body and the core for the force of power of the stroke.

SHOULDER - STEP 8

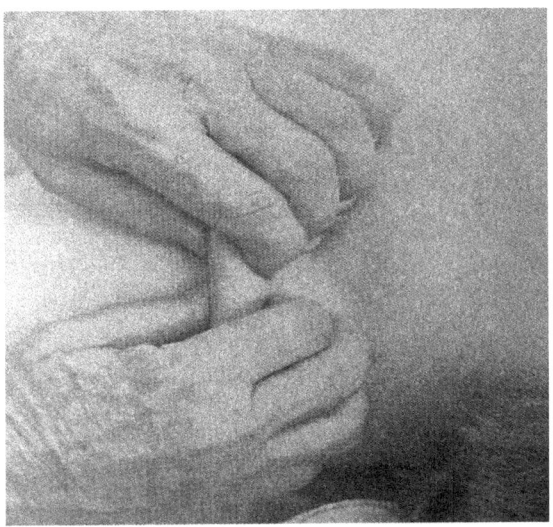

This move is skin rolling or skin lifting. This move can be uncomfortable for the patient/client if applied improperly. Use the fingers and the thumbs to raise the tissue up and toward you. Release the tissue and repeat the move. You may move in any direction. This is a common move that can be utilized in most body areas: shoulder, mid and low back, hip, thigh, and leg. So, remember to consider this move when you're working in these areas. Again, this move can be very uncomfortable for the patient/client if applied aggressively. Work slowly and lightly at first and add pressure as needed, working within a tolerable comfort range. Remember to utilize the core and body to provide the power for the stroke, not the fingers, thumbs, hands, or arms.

SHOULDER - STEP 9

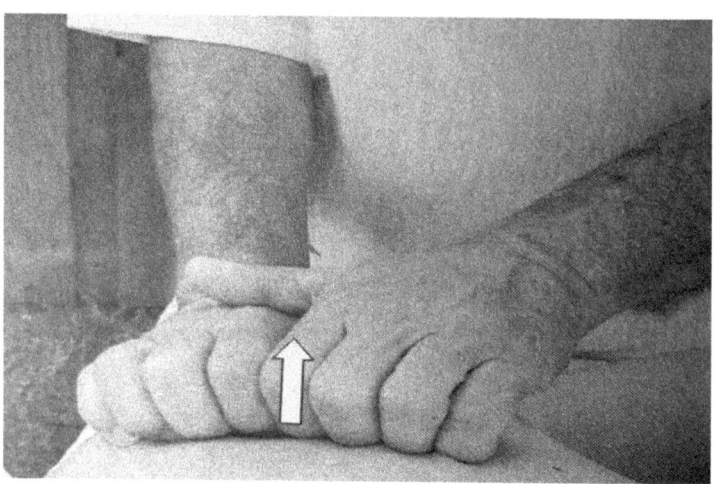

This move is called the scapula pull. Curl the fingers of both hands and place them under the medial scapula, lifting it with light pressure. Then, crouch and pull back with your body while pulling the scapula upward. Do not pull with your fingers and hands; rather, let the weight of your backward-leaning body do the work. This will feel less aggressive to the patient/client. Work slowly and deliberately. Pressure for this particular move will remain constant.

SHOULDER - STEP 10

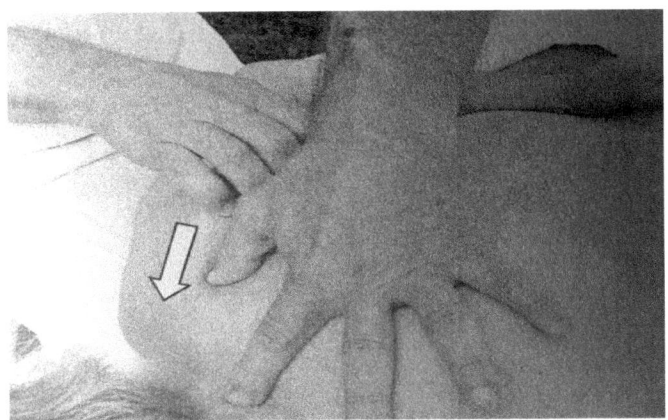

In this illustration, we see the rhomboid stretch by pulling laterally back on the scapula. Run the thumb under the medial border of the scapula, working from inferior to superior. Also, you will be able to obtain more access to the scapula border if the same arm and hand of the patient/client are placed on her back. Use body weight and core to apply force for the stroke. Move slowly, starting with light pressure and adding pressure as needed, working in a tolerable comfort range.

SHOULDER - STEP 11

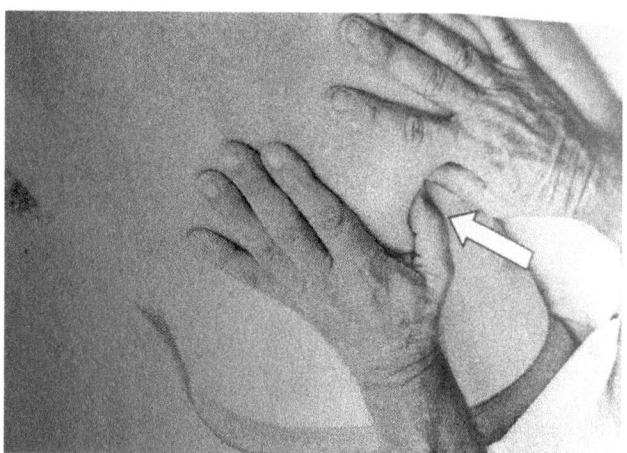

Utilize the thumbs to compress the areas of the teres and subscapularis muscles. Use the core and body weight to apply force, not the thumbs, for this move. Work slowly and add pressure as needed. Work within a tolerable comfort range. Be careful working in this area since you are close to the axillary endangerment site.

SHOULDER - STEP 12

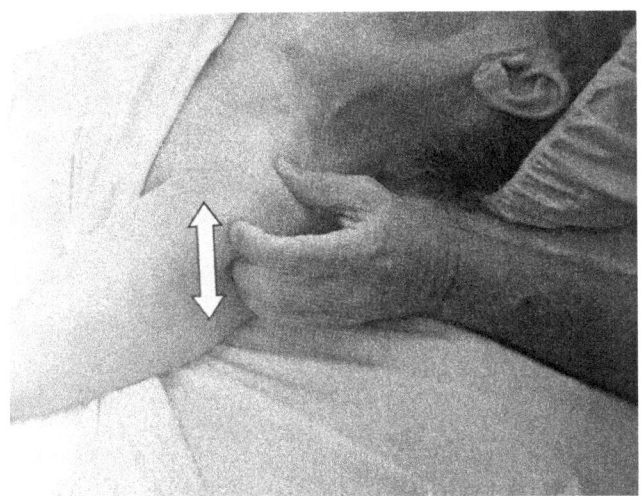

    With the fingers, use a back-and-forth anterior to posterior - posterior to anterior motion, applying friction to the attachment area of the SITS muscles. The stroke is performed from a seated position for the best and most comfortable for the therapist. You may rest your arm on the table for added support and this will help keep it in a relaxed state. This is the joint area, so be very careful. Even though this is a mild move remember to utilize the body and core for the force of the stroke.

UPPER - MID BACK STEP 1

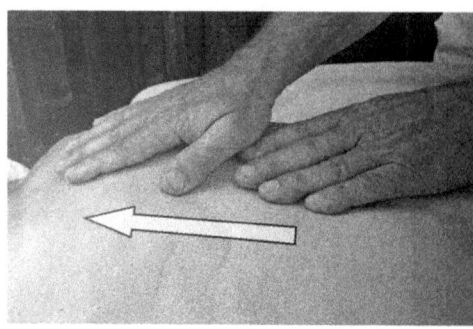

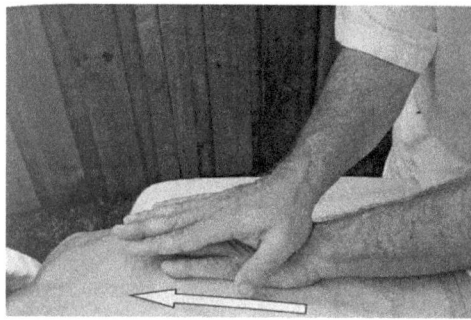

This is a repeat of the hand behindhand, supported hand on hand, and slide and glide positions found in shoulder step 2, page 49 above. This time, you will be focusing on the following muscle groups: lower - mid traps and paraspinals. Work slowly and deliberately, starting with a light touch, adding pressure as needed staying within a tolerable comfort range. Remember, the force of stroke comes from the body and core.

UPPER - MID BACK STEP 2

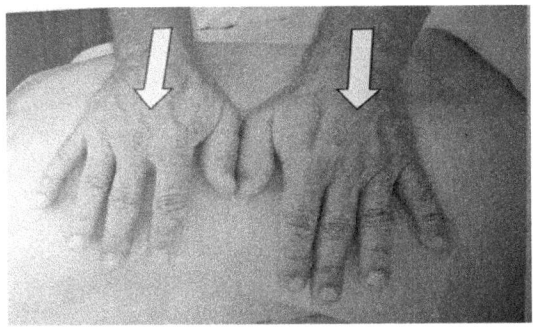

This stroke is pushing with the palms of the hands, producing a stretch and hold. The direction is medial to lateral, away from the spine. Work up and down - down and up, affecting the paraspinal. Use the weight of the body in order to produce the force of stroke. Work slowly, deliberately and lightly at first, adding pressure as needed, staying within a tolerable comfort range. Do not apply major force in this stroke since it is a stretch. Do not apply any pressure directly on the spine.

UPPER - MID BACK STEP 3

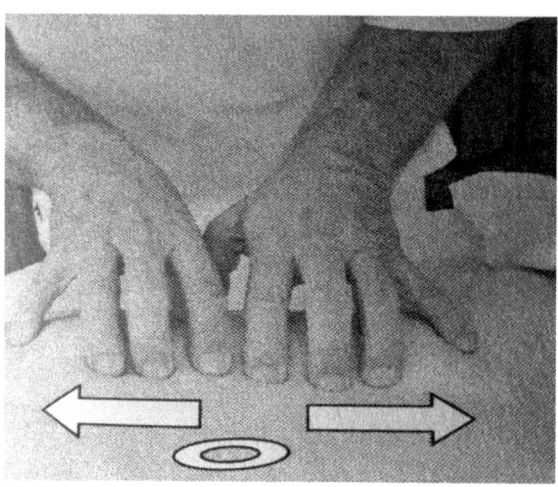

Move the fingers up and down the paraspinal area, and as you move, use a light circular friction motion. Also, you can use a raking motion, pulling back slightly, medial to lateral, as you go up and down the paraspinal. You will be working in the lamina groove area of the back. Work slowly and deliberately, using only as much pressure as needed and staying within a tolerable comfort range. Use the body and core to provide the force of the stroke.

UPPER - MID BACK STEP 4

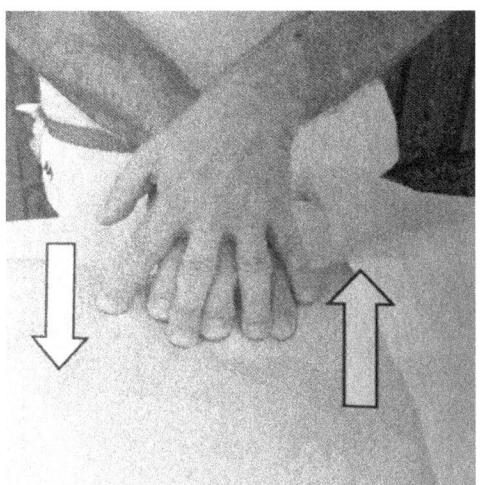

This move makes use of both hands simultaneously, performing a stretch in the lamina groove- paraspinal areas. The bottom hand moves laterally while the top hand holds medially. This will stretch the paraspinal as you move up and down the lamina groove. Work slowly and with deliberation, staying within a tolerable comfort range. Utilize the body and core to provide the power for the stroke.

UPPER - MID BACK STEP 5

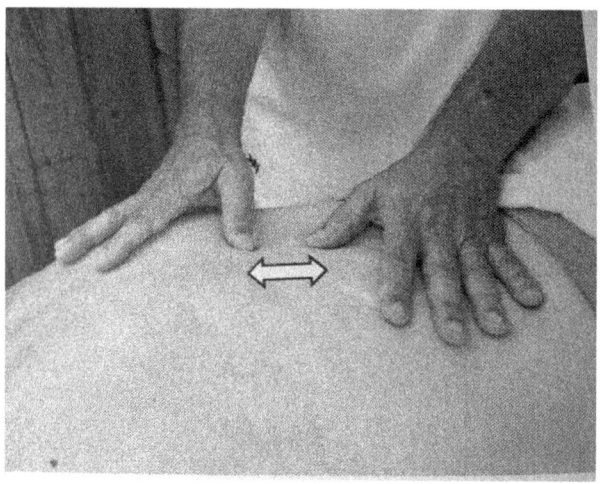

Step 5 is similar to step 4 in that it is a stretch; however, you will utilize only the thumbs. You will move medial and lateral and up and down the paraspinal - lamina groove areas. The thumb moving laterally performs the stretch while the medial thumb holds. Work slowly, as well as deliberately, adding pressure as needed while working in a tolerable comfort range. Use the body and core to provide the power for the stroke. This is a type of myofascial stroke.

UPPER - MID BACK STEP 6

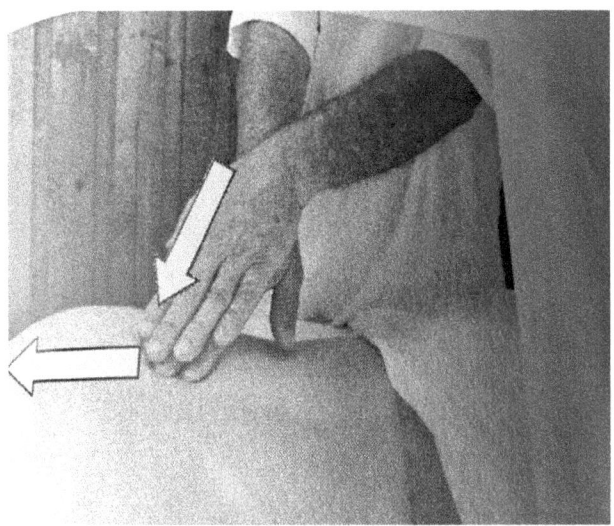

In this move you will use the fingers to apply a sliding stroke going from inferior to superior along the lamina groove - paraspinal regions. This is a supported hand-finger position placing one hand over the other to help add pressure to the stroke. Remember to use the body and core to produce the force of stroke. Work slowly and deliberately and work within a tolerable comfort range. Keep the wrist as straight as possible.

UPPER - MID BACK STEP 7

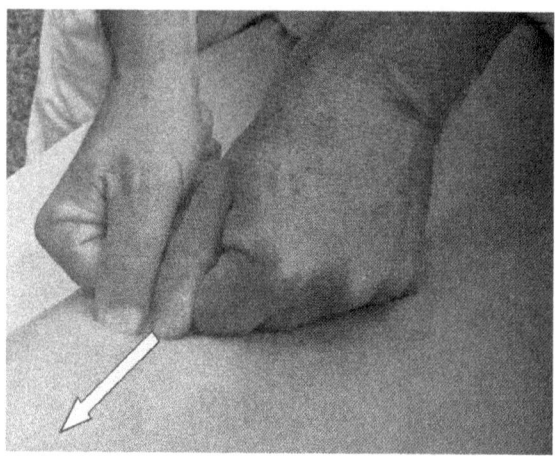

This is a sliding move using supported thumbs. You will be working the erector spinae group, lats and traps. Work slowly and deliberately. Start with light pressure and add pressure as needed, always working within a tolerable comfort range. Utilize the body and core to apply stroke force. The fists can also help to broaden the tissue as you move through the stroke. Work in an inferior to superior direction.

UPPER - MID BACK STEP 8

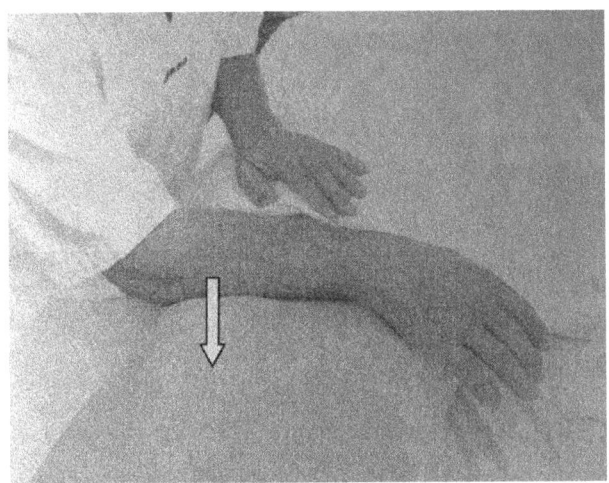

This stroke is applied using the forearm over the back area. You will be working in the direction of inferior to superior. Use the meat of the arm, not the bony part. Start with light pressure and add pressure as needed while always working within a tolerable comfort range. Use the body and core to apply the force of the stroke. Work slowly and deliberately. Make sure the hand of the arm performing the stroke is relaxed during the movement. If the hand is relaxed, the arm, shoulder, neck, and back will also be relaxed, ensuring that the stroke will not be aggressive.

UPPER - MID BACK STEP 9

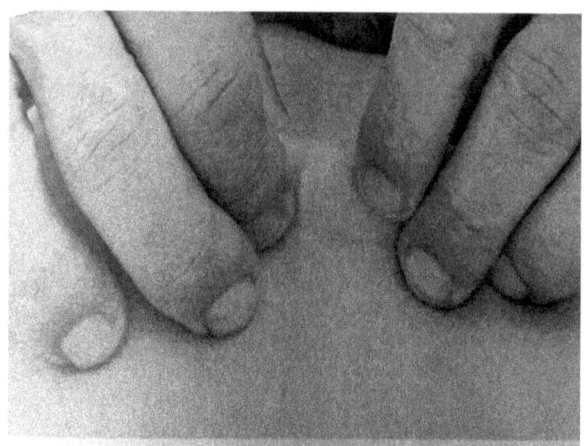

Skin rolling is a good move for the scapula area. Refer to page 55, Shoulder - Step 8 above for directions.

UPPER MID - BACK STEP 10

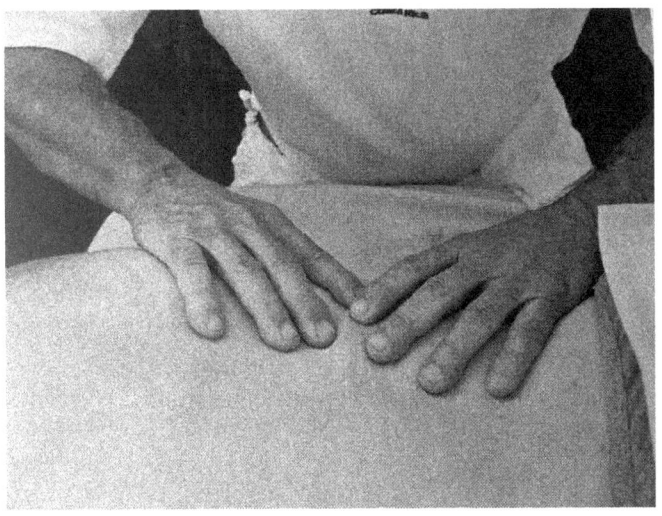

This is a standard petrissage move. This move can be used with effleurage after the other moves are completed to help loosen and flush out toxins. Work slowly and deliberately and stay within a tolerable comfort range. Force of the stroke should come from the body and the core.

UPPER - MID BACK STEP 11 AND LOW BACK STEP 1

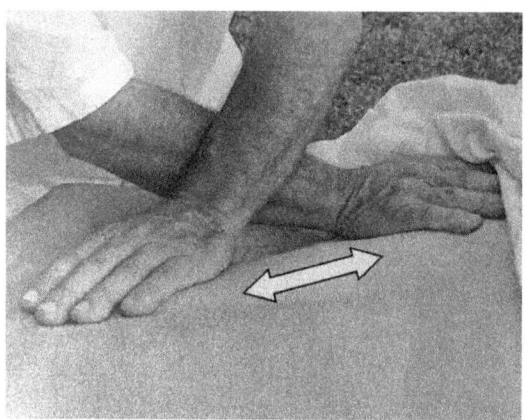

This move is called cross-handed myofascial stretch. This can be used in both Mid – Upper Back and Low Back areas. This move helps to take pressure off the wrists and arms. Work slowly and deliberately, staying within tolerable comfort range. Use the body and core to provide the force for the stroke.

LOW - BACK STEP 2a

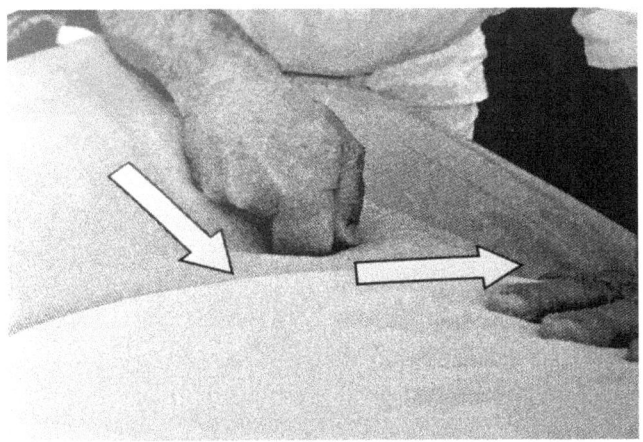

LOW - BACK STEP 2b

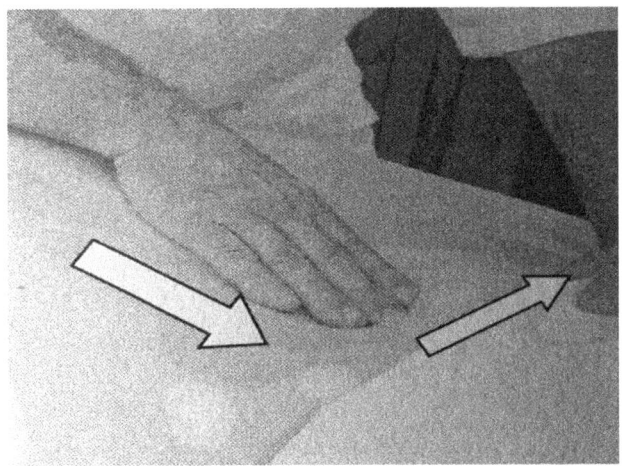

This move concentrates on the quadratus lumborum, also. This time, you will work with the supported forefinger knuckle or the fingers and palm of the hand, moving down the lamina groove into the iliac crest. This is also a slide-and-glide move. Work slowly and deliberately increasing pressure as needed, staying within a tolerable and comfortable range.

LOW - BACK STEP 3

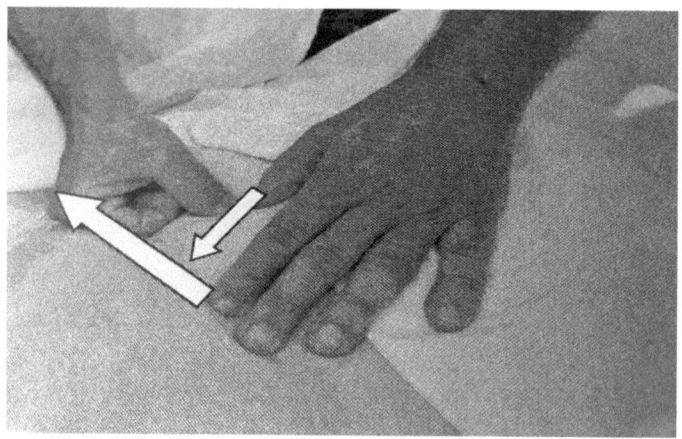

This move incorporates both thumbs in a slide/glide move over the iliac crest attachment. You will move slightly in an inferior to superior direction from the gluteal area to the iliac crest. When you reach the crest, move medial to lateral with a glide and slide move. This will loosen fibers, break up adhesions, and flush toxins. Keep the wrist straight and use the body and core to provide the force of the stroke. Work slowly and deliberately. Start with light pressure, gradually increasing it as needed, always staying within a tolerable comfort range.

LOW - BACK STEP 4

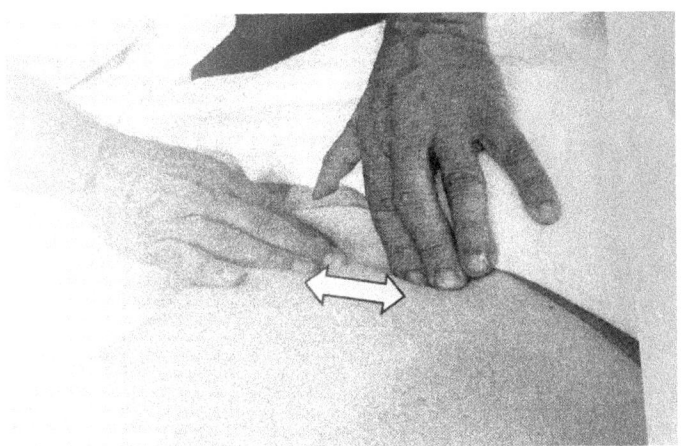

This move incorporates the use of the index finger and middle finger of each hand with the application of friction. You will concentrate on the attachment of the floating rib of the quadratus lumborum. This movement requires only a light touch. There is no need to be aggressive in this situation. Work slowly and deliberately and even if working with a light touch, use the body and the core to generate the energy for this move. This move will loosen the toxins that collect in this area.

HIP - STEP 1

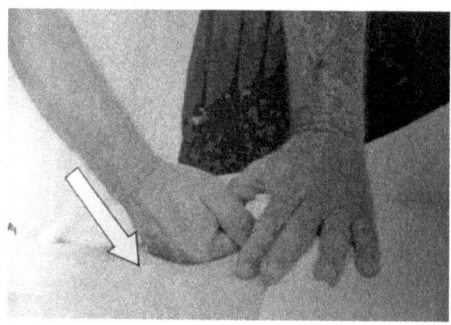 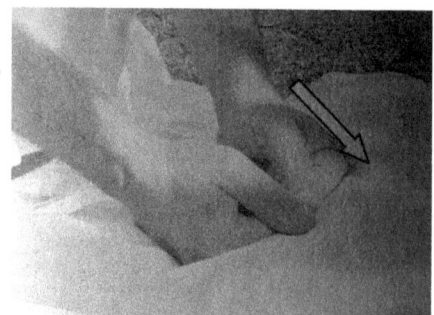

In this move we are working in the gluteal area of the hip. The application is compression using the fist. You may use one hand or two; it is your decision. At the end of each compression give a little twist of the fist. Work slowly and deliberately. Start with a light pressure and increase as needed, always working within a tolerable comfort range. Circle the entire gluteal area for this movement. Remember to use the body and core for the force of the stroke. For the purpose of modesty, work through a sheet or towel covering the gluteal area. Keep the wrist straight.

HIP - STEP 2

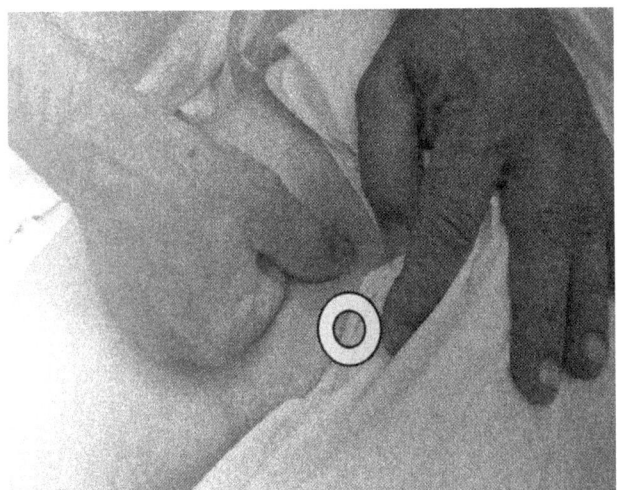

In this illustration we are using the supported thumb to apply circular friction. In this case, it is being used in joint areas, such as the trochanter and piriformis attachments in the area of the hip. Start with light pressure and increase as needed, always working within a tolerable comfort range. Be conscious of using the body and core for the force of the stroke. Work slowly and deliberately. This move is beneficial in that it will loosen and flush toxins from the area.

HIP - STEP 3

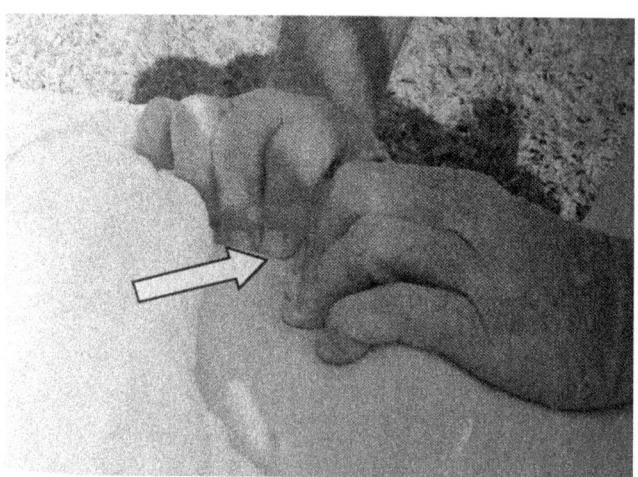

In this move, you will be using both hands, fingers, and palms. You will grab the fascia with your fingers and palms. The application is called skin (FASCIA) stretching. After securing the fascia, pull with the body weight for the force of the stroke, hold, and release. This stroke is best used in the larger muscle areas, such as the glutes. Use light pressure at first, increasing as needed, always working within a tolerable comfort range. Work slowly and deliberately.

THIGH - STEP 1

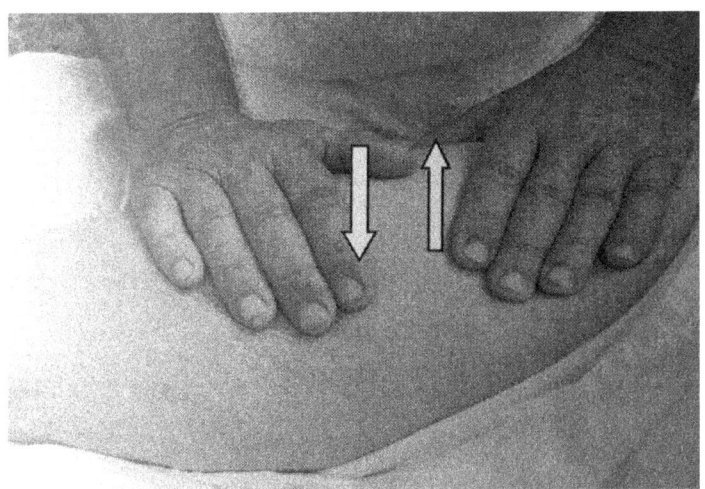

This is a friction stroke moving the fascia tissue in two different directions simultaneously. Start with light pressure, adding pressure as needed and working within a tolerable comfort range. As you progress in the move, it can become a stretch and hold. Always work slowly and deliberately. Again, use the body and core for the force of the stroke. In this move we are focused on the hamstrings.

THIGH - STEP 2

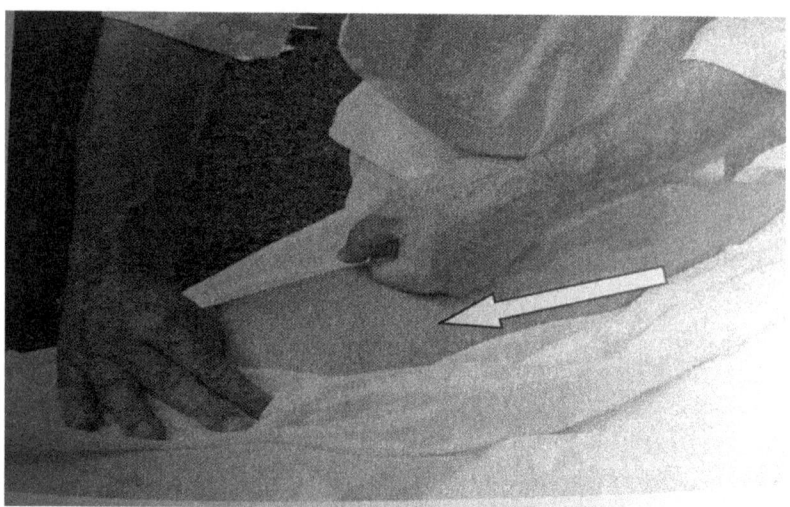

Use the fist in a slide and glide move along the hamstring in the direction of distal to proximal. You will be able to loosen the fibers of this tissue. Start with light pressure and increase as needed, always working within a tolerable comfort range. Use the body and core to generate the power for the stroke. Work slowly and deliberately. As you begin this move you may add a slight compression before you start slide and glide.

THIGH - STEP 3

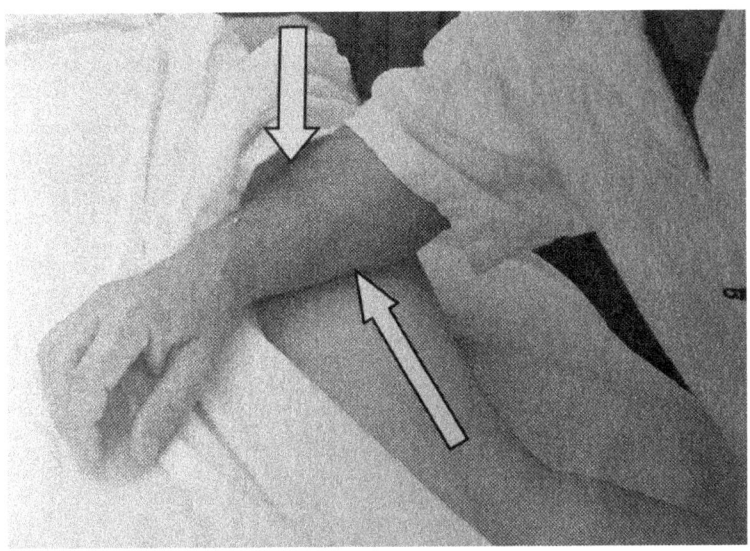

Once again, we see the use of the forearm. The pressure is down while sliding from distal to proximal on the thigh. The hand remains relaxed during the move so as not to cause rigidity in your upper extremity, shoulder, and neck. Pressure will be light at first and increasing as needed, however, stay within a tolerable comfort range. Work slowly and deliberately. Utilize the body and core to generate the power for the stroke.

THIGH - STEP 4

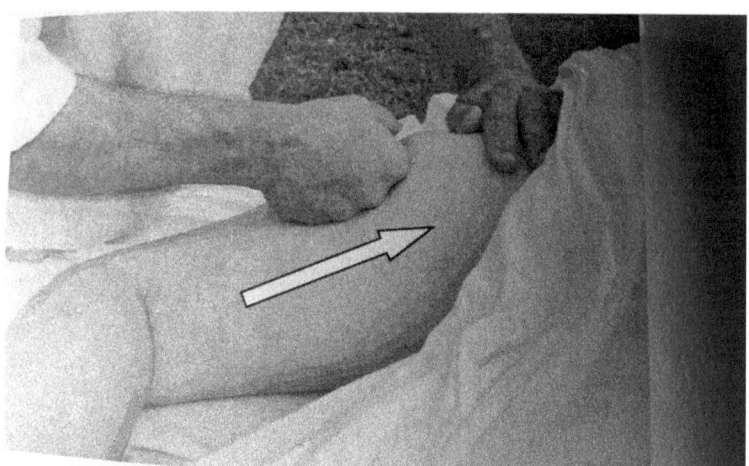

This is a slide-and-glide move utilizing the fist. The patient is lying on her side. We are focusing on the I.T. band and TFL. You will move inferior to superior along the I.T. band. You will apply light pressure at first and gradually increase the pressure as needed, always working within the tolerable comfort range. Slowly and deliberately. Use the body and core to generate the power for the stroke. As an added note, I have always found that working with a very light touch in this area produced better results than using aggressive pressure.

THIGH - STEP 5

a   b

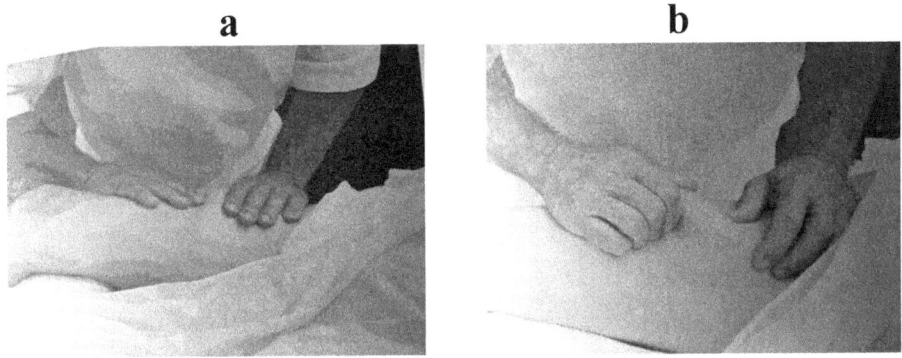

In these two illustrations, see examples of types of skin lifting. For example **a,** we apply the skin lifting by bringing both hands together and raising the fascia up between the hands. In example **b,** we applied the skin lifting with the thumb and forefinger of each hand and then form an S shape with the hands pulling and pushing in opposite directions. Start with a light pressure, adding pressure as needed, and only work within a tolerable comfort range. Use the body and core to provide the force for the stroke. Work slowly and deliberately. These strokes can be used in other parts of the body, such as the back, shoulder, and leg. This move can loosen and remove toxins from the area, as well as relax the fascia. The routine for hamstrings and quads is basically the same.

LEG - STEP 1

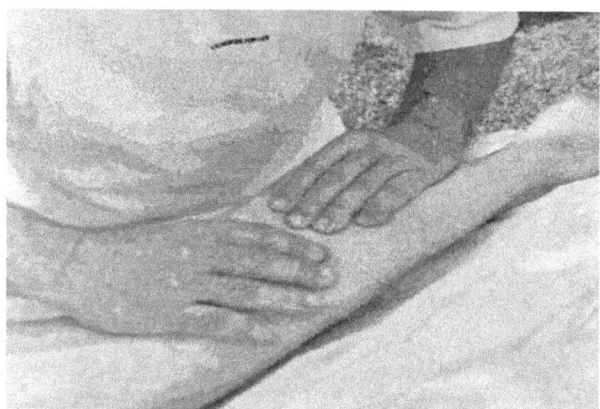

Start the leg routine with standard petrissage to help loosen and warm the two muscles, soleus, and gastrocnemius, and to help flush toxins from the area. Work slowly and deliberately. Begin with light pressure, adding pressure as needed, always staying within a tolerable comfort range. Feel free to use petrissage in any of the larger muscle groups, as well.

LEG - STEP 2

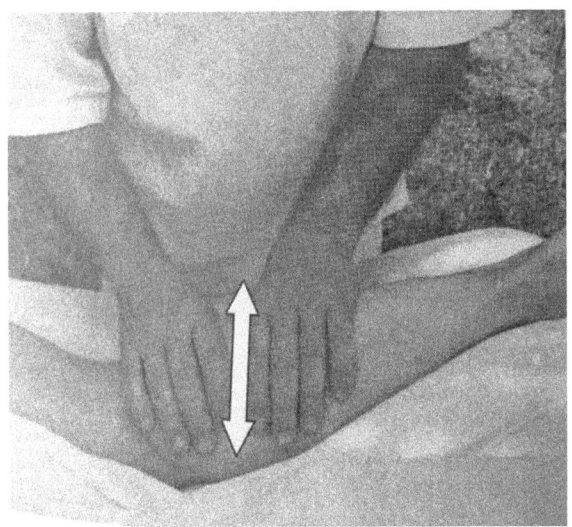

This move is called stretch and hold. You will be utilizing both hands, placing them on the calf area with palms down as if playing a piano. You will move the hands simultaneously, in opposite directions, as if ringing. After each stretch, you will hold for a few seconds. This move will help to break up restrictions that may exist in the fascia. Work slowly and deliberately. Start with light pressure, adding pressure as needed, staying within a tolerable comfort range. Use the body and the core to provide the power for the stroke. This stroke may be used on the arms, thighs, and the legs.

LEG - STEP 3

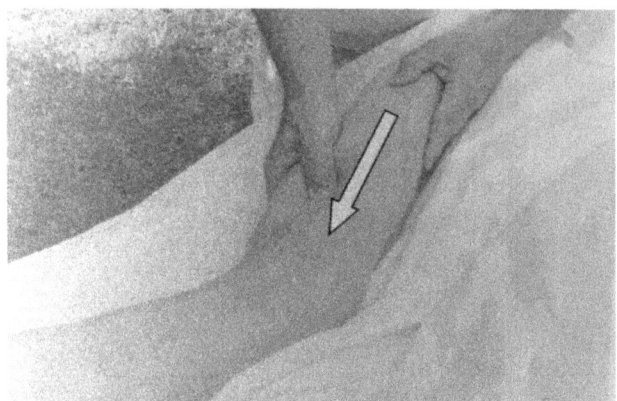

In this move, you will apply stripping with an unsupported thumb. You will be working from distal to proximal in the gastrocnemius and soleus muscles. You will be supporting the leg with the other hand. Work slowly and deliberately. Start with light pressure and add pressure as needed, staying within a tolerable comfort range. Focus on providing power from the core and body as an energy source for the stroke.

LEG - STEP 4

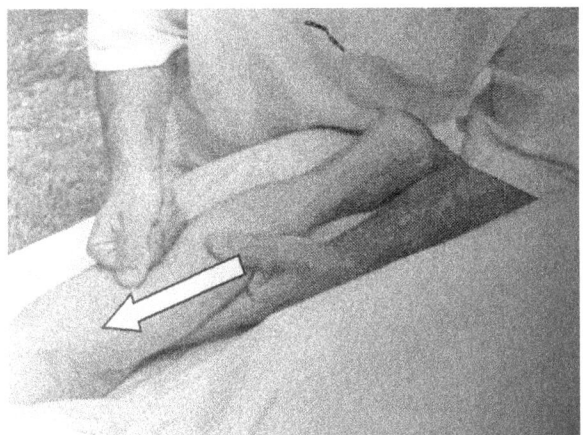

This move incorporates the use of the fist to support the thumb, as well as provide a slide and glide application, along with stripping with the supported thumb. You will move in the direction of distal to proximal in the gastrocnemius and soleus muscles. Start with light pressure, adding more pressure as needed, staying within a tolerable comfort range. Utilize the body and core to produce the energy for the force of the stroke. Work slowly and deliberately.

LEG - STEP 5

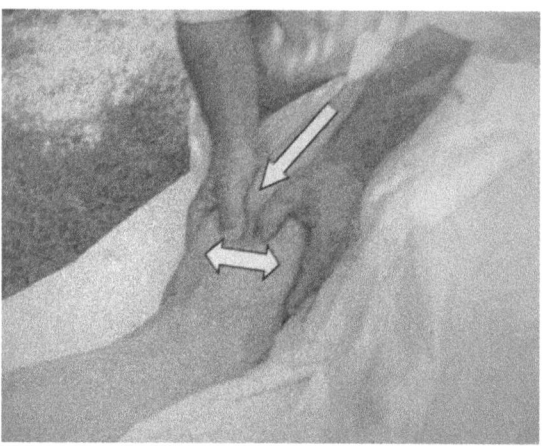

This move incorporates a slide and glide and broadening. You will run the length of the soleus and gastrocnemius muscles, working from distal to proximal. Work slowly and deliberately. Start with light pressure, adding pressure as needed, staying within a tolerable comfort range. Use the body and core to generate the energy for the force of the stroke. Steps 3, 4, and 5 will help to break up adhesions and relax the muscles and fascia, which will, in turn, promote the circulation of blood, lymph, and nervous systems. This enhances muscle and fascia nutrition, detoxification, and mobility.

LEG - STEP 6

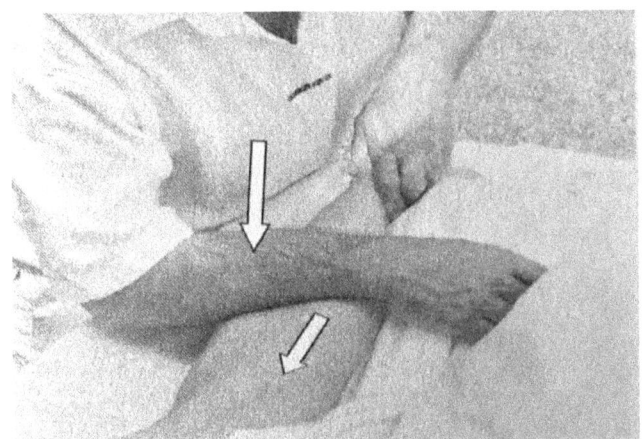

This illustration shows the use of the forearm as a form of compression and slide/glide. You will work in the direction of distal to proximal. Work slowly and deliberately. Start with light pressure, adding pressure as needed, making sure to stay within a tolerable comfort range. Use the body and core to generate the energy needed to perform the stroke.

ADDITIONAL PHOTOS ILLUSTRATING BODY AND HAND-ARM FORM

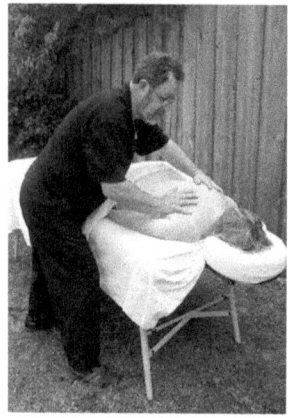

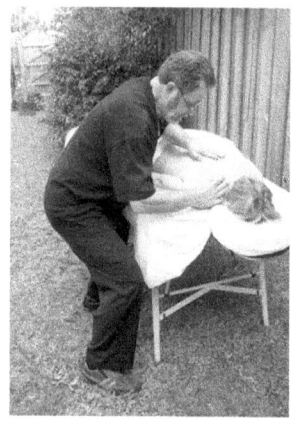

Note the stances emulate the Tai Chi and Qi Gong stances, lunging, crouching, leaning, and using the body and core to generate the force for the massage applications.

Chapter Eight:
Anatomic Illustrations

Anatomical Considerations Relative to Working with
JIN MO QI GONG

This chapter presents anatomy relative to the areas illustrated in chapter seven. Along with a comprehensive muscle group list (refer to page 41), valuable, relevant data is offered for consideration, such as the location of muscle, attachment locations, and muscle action symptomatology. It is my hope that the following information will enhance your learning experience by combining the more traditional massage data with the less traditional teachings found in the JIN MO QI GONG method.

Anatomical Considerations

A. Identification of common injury areas and causes that may benefit

from JIN MO Qi GONG

NOTES:

Neck - can do deep work but needs to be especially careful

Shoulder - some muscles here are part of the upper back and neck

Trunk - primarily low back and mid back

Hip - strong connection with the lower back and lower extremity (thigh)

Lower Extremity - thigh and leg, big, strong muscles; caution in the area of the femoral triangle

General symptoms: pain, tightness, stiffness, soreness, impaired ROM, tenderness,

General causes: work, leisure, home, sports, poor posture, overuse, overexertion, lack of exercise, overweight, auto accident, misuse of muscle, poor sleeping positions, toxicity.

B. Anatomy of the common injury areas that may benefit from JIN MO QI GONG

a. Neck

b. Shoulder

c. Upper Back and Lower Back

d. Hip

e. Lower Extremities

C. Review of muscle charts and supporting data

Notes:

Val Nardo

THE NECK

STERNOCLEIDOMASTOID

SCALENES

Muscle Name: Sternocleidomastoid (SCM)

Attachments:

O-Sternal Head and Clavicular Head

I- Mastoid of Temporal Bone

Actions:

Bilateral - Flex neck forward

Unilateral - Lateral flex of neck on the same side

Rotation of head on opposite side and upward

Common injuries/symptoms: headache, neck pain, stiff neck

Common causes: whiplash - auto accident, sleeping improperly or poor pillow, prolonged sitting at the computer looking up or down

Notes:

Sternocleidomastoid

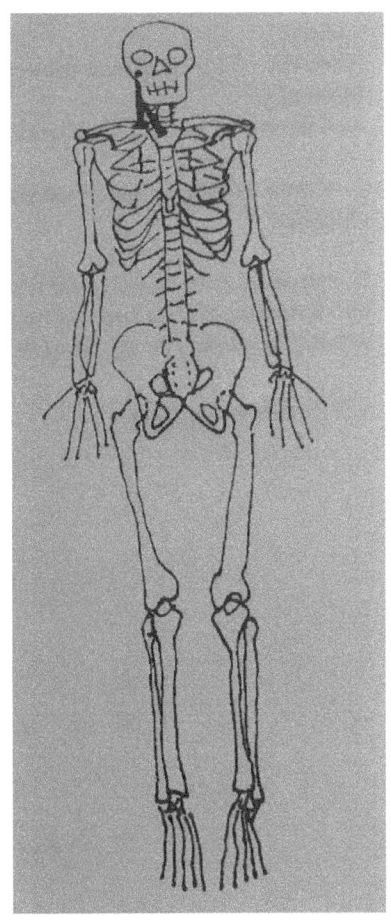

Muscle Name: Scalenes

Attachments:

O-Transverse Processes of Cervical Vertebrae

C2-C7, Med., Ant., Post.

1 - Anterior and Medius of 1" Rib and Posterior of 2nd Rib

Action:

Bilateral - Flex neck and raise 1st rib during strong

Inhalation Unilateral - Lateral flex of the neck and rotates the neck

Common injuries/symptoms: pain in neck, arm, and shoulder

Common causes: hypertonic muscles placing pressure on *Brachial Plexus and *Subclavian artery, any activity requiring strong breathing

Notes:

Scalenes

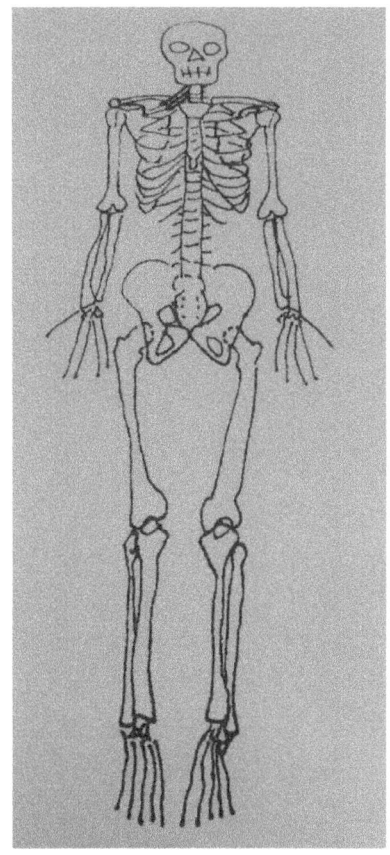

Val Nardo

SHOULDER

TRAPEZIUS

LEVATOR SCAPULA

RHOMBOIDS

LATISSIMUS DORSI

SUBSCAPULARIS

SUPRASPINATUS

INFRASPINATUS

TERES MINOR

Muscle Name: Trapezius

Attachments:

O- Base of Occiput and Spinous Processes at C7 and T1-T12

I- Lateral3rd of Clavicle, Acromium Processes, and Spine of Scapula

Action:

Upper - Elevates shoulder girdle, prevents depression of girdle when wgt. Carried on the shoulder or in the hands

Middle - Adducts scapula (retraction)

Lower - Depresses scapula against resistance when getting up from chair while using arms and hands.

Upper and Lower - Rotates scapula while elevating arm overhead

Common injuries/symptoms: upper traps - neck pain, neck stiffness, headaches, rounded shoulders

Common causes: overuse in sports, such as rowing; overuse in work activity, such as painting overhead or working overhead; prolonged and improper holding of the phone; carrying a heavy purse heavy backpack; sitting too long without an armrest on a chair, armrest on a chair too high; improperly placed computer screen

Notes:

Trapezius

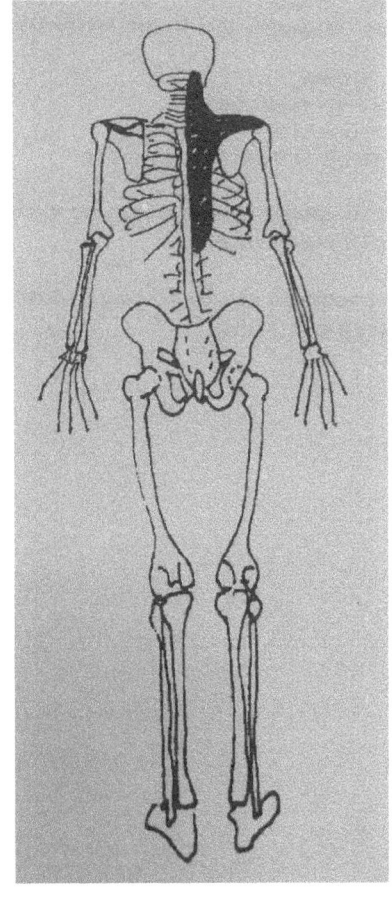

Muscle Name: Levator Scapula

Attachments:

O-Transverse Processes C1 -C4

I - Upper Medial Vertebral Border of Scapula

Action:

Elevates scapula Helps to retract scapula Helps to bend neck laterally

Common injuries/symptoms: neck pain, neck stiffness, headaches

Common causes: carrying or lifting objects too heavy, as in weight lifting

Notes:

Levator Scapula

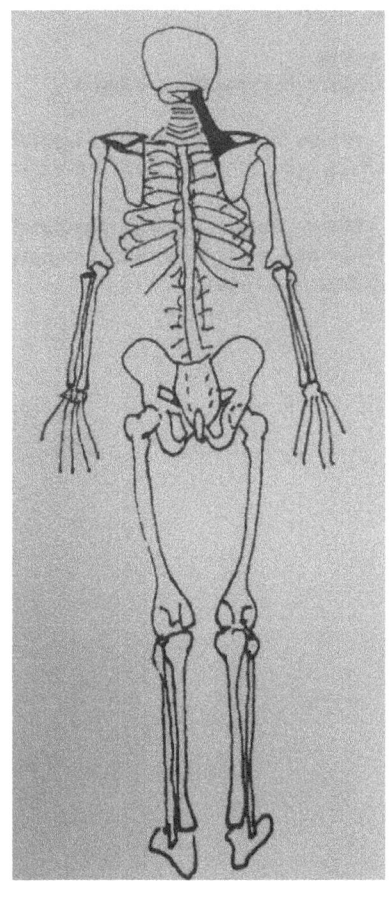

Muscle Name: Rhomboid Minor

Attachments:

O - Spinous Processes C7-T-1

I - Upper ½ of the Medial Border of the Scapula

Action:

Adducts and stabilizes scapula

Common injuries/symptoms: tightness, soreness, aching between scapulae, rounded shoulders

Common causes: over-stretched and overuse of rhomboids in sports activity, such as racket sports, archery, and rowing

Notes:

Rhomboid Minor

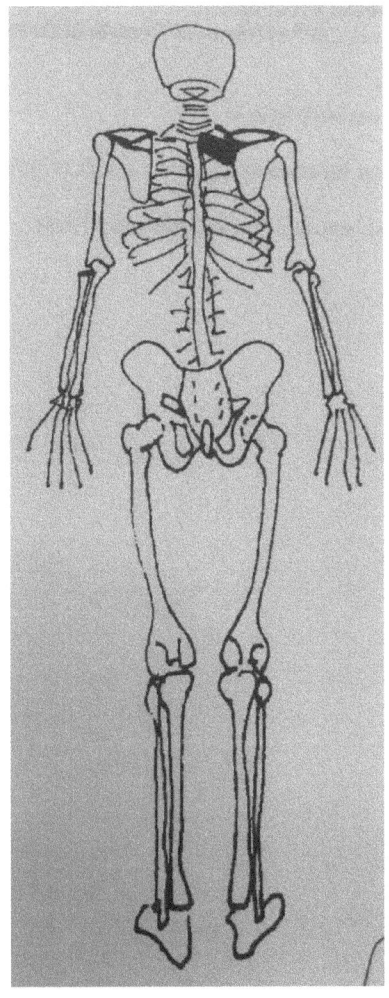

Muscle Name: Rhomboid Major

Attachments:

O-Spinous Processes T1 - T5

I- Lower 2/3rd of Medical Vertebral Border of Scapula

Action:

See Rhomboid Minor

Common injuries/symptoms: see Rhomboid Minor

Common causes: see Rhomboid Minor

Notes:

Rhomboid Major

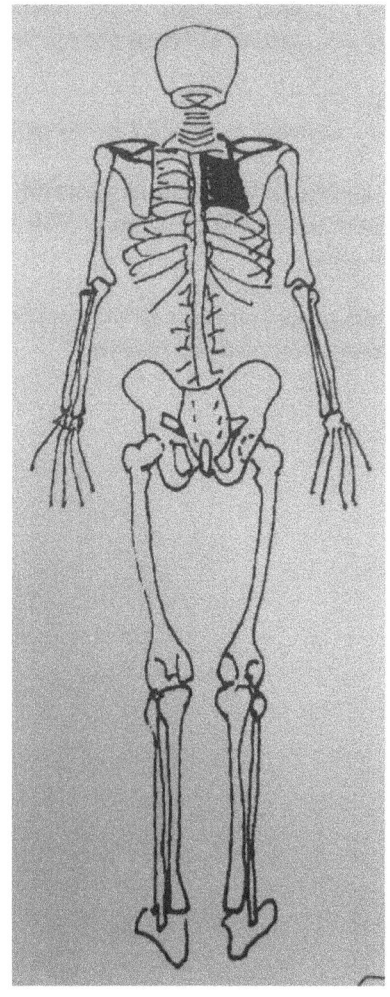

Muscle Name: Latissimus Dorsi

Attachments:

O-Spinous Processes of T7 - S5, Posterior of Iliac Crest, Lower 3-4 Ribs, Inferior Angle of Scapula I - Bicipital Groove of Humerus just below shoulder joint

Action:

Extends, adducts, and rotates humerus medially

Common injuries/symptoms: generally mild pain. Muscles are superficial to other back muscles that may have a relationship to back pain.

Common causes: overuse or overstretching in activities, such as gardening, water skiing, painting

Notes:

Latissimus Dorsi

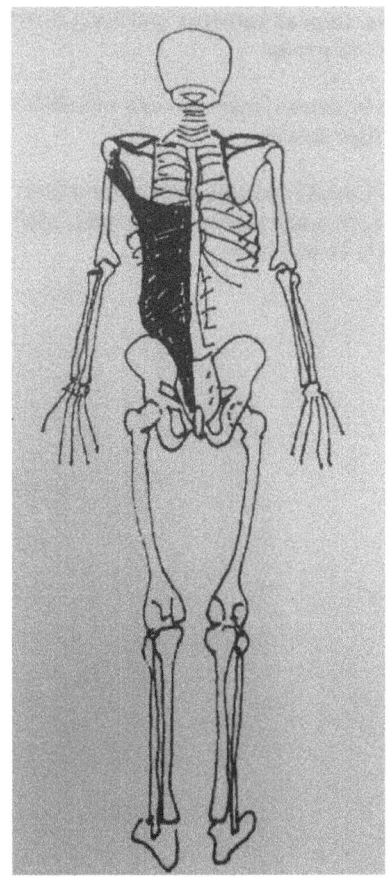

Muscle Name: Subscapularis

Attachments:

O-Anterior Surface of Scapula

I-Lesser Tubercle of Humerus

Action:

Medial rotation of the humerus and stabilizes shoulder joint, part of the SITS group

Common injuries/symptoms: cannot abduct arm, round shoulder posture, tight muscle

Common causes: twisting arm behind back in an attempt to catch self in a fall, overzealous restraining hold, pitching a baseball overhead, and craw stroke in swimming

Notes:

Subscapularis

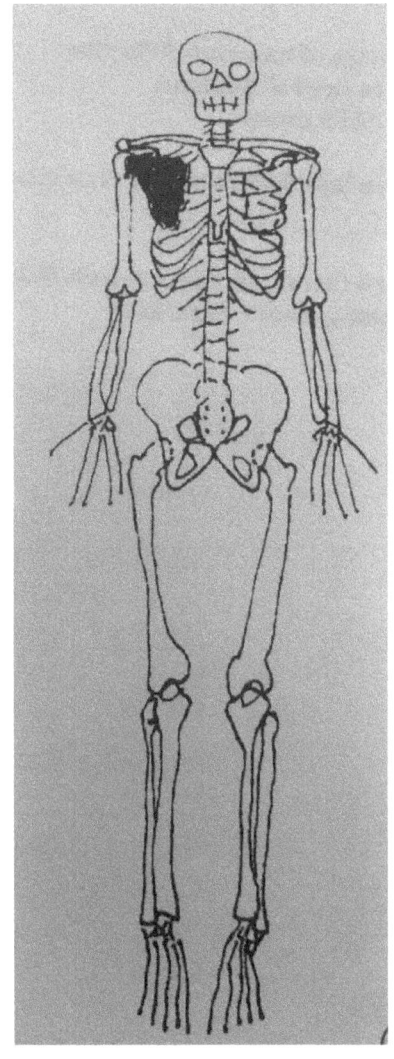

Muscle Name: Supraspinatus

Attachments:

O - Supraspinatus Fossa of Scapula

I- Greater Tubercle of Humerus

Action:

The initial stage of humerus abduction stabilizes the head of the humerus, which is part of the SITS group.

Common injuries/symptoms: can mimic bursitis,

Common causes: carrying objects that are too heavy or beyond a person's capability

Notes:

Supraspinatus

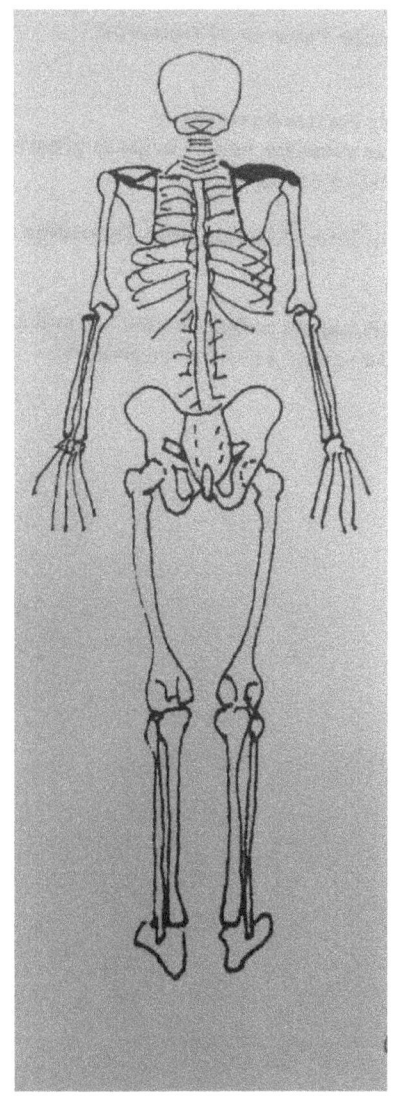

Muscle Name: Infraspinatus

Attachments:

O - Middle 2/3rd of Posterior side of Scapula below Spine of Scapula

I-Greater Tubercle of Humerus

Action:

Laterally rotates humerus

Stabilizes shoulder joint - helps to prevent dislocation. Part of the SITS group.

Common injuries/symptoms: dislocation of shoulder, shoulder pain

Common causes: falling backward and catching yourself with your arm, polling in skiing, miss-hit tennis serve

Notes:

Infraspinatus

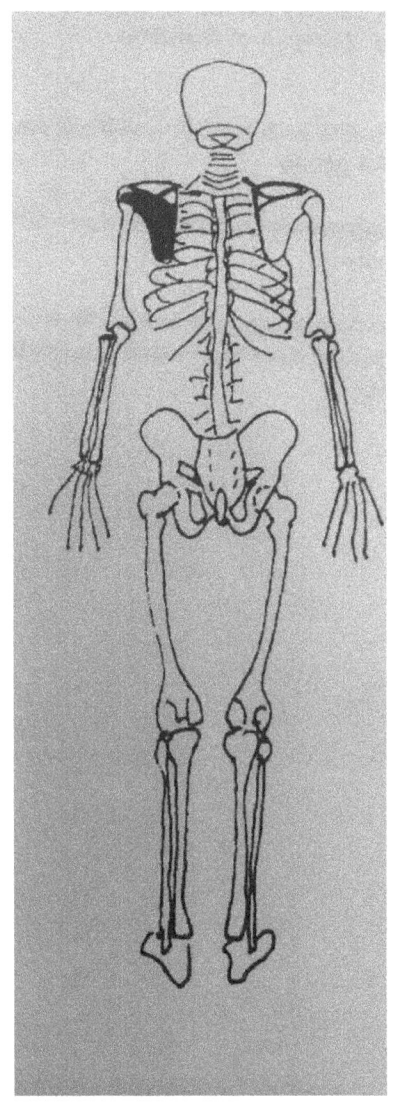

Muscle Name: Teres Minor

Attachments:

O - Upper Axillary Border of Scapula

I-Greater Tubercle of Humerus

Action:

Lateral rotation and extension of humerus Part of SITS group

Common injuries/symptoms: shoulder dislocation, shoulder pain

Common causes: placing arm in back to catch self in a fall, excessive polling in skiing, miss-hitting a tennis serve

Notes:

Teres Minor

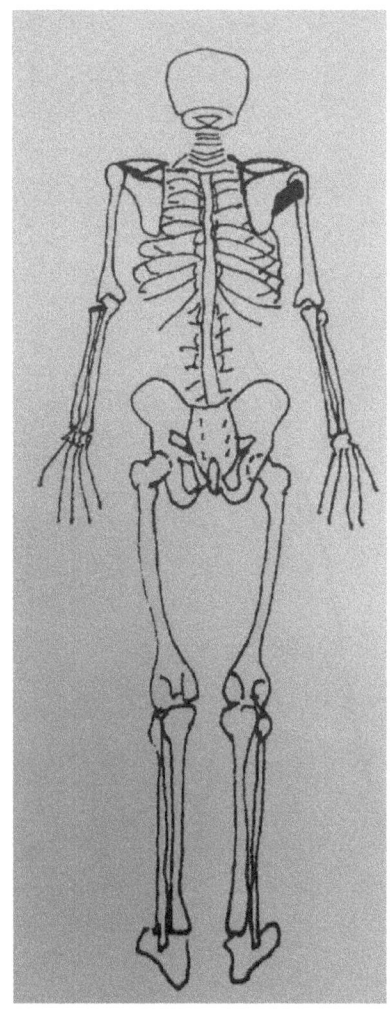

Val Nardo

UPPER-MID-LOWER BACK

ROTATORES

MULTIFIDI

LONGISSIMUS

ILIOCOSTALIS

QUADRATUS LUMBORUM

Muscle Name: *Rotators

Attachments:

O-Transverse Process of each Vertebra

I - Base of each Spinous Process adjoining the above Vertebra

Action:

Bilateral - extension of spine

Unilateral - rotation to opposite side

Common injuries/symptoms: strain, sprain, local pain, soreness, tightness

Common causes: lifting without bending knees, lifting without keeping back erect, lifting an object too far from the front of the body

Notes:

Rotatores

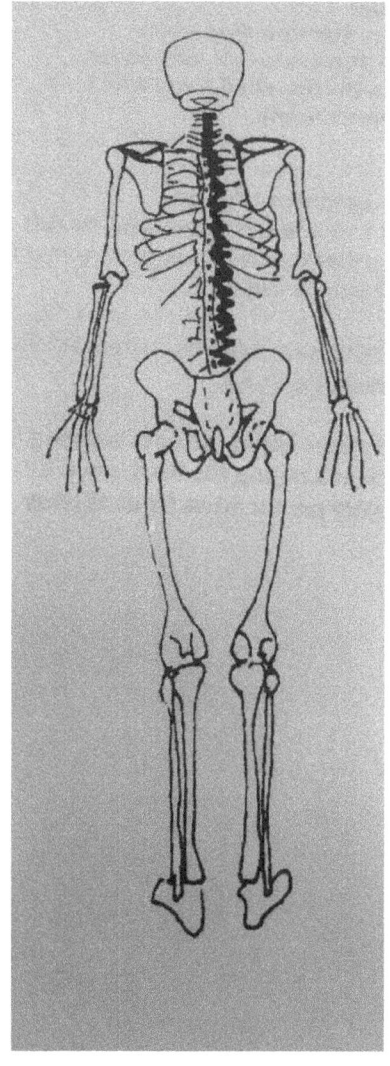

Muscle Name: Multifidi

Attachments:

O-Sacrum, Superior Iliac Spine

Transverse Processes - all Vertebrae

I- Spinous Process of all Vertebrae 2 - 4 Vertebra above origin

Action:

Bilateral - extension of spine

Unilateral - rotation of spine on opposite side Protects vertebral joints from more powerful superficial muscle action.

Common injuries/symptoms: strain, strain, local pain, soreness, tightness

Common causes: lifting without bending the knees, lifting without keeping the back erect, lifting while holding the object too far from the front of the body

Notes:

Multifidi

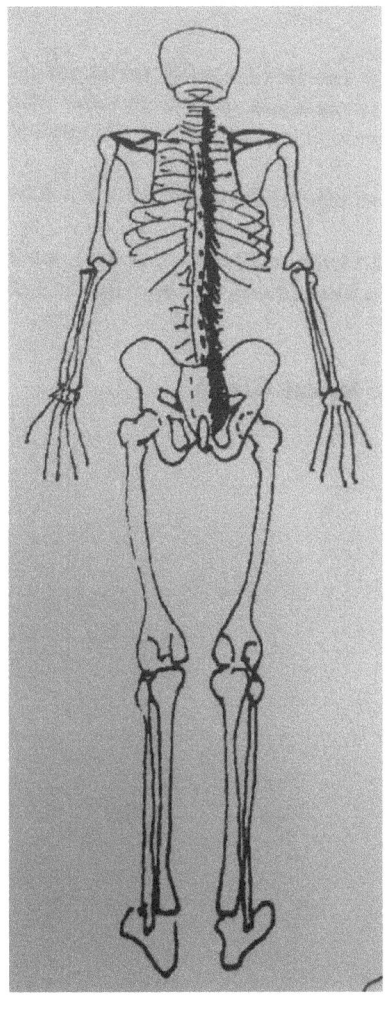

Muscle Name: *Spinalis

Attachments:

O- Spinous Processes of Cervical and Thoracic Vertebrae

I - Transverse Processes of Cervical and Thoracic Vertebrae

Action:

Extends and flexes laterally vertebral column Helps to maintain spine curvature while standing and sitting Stabilizes vertebral column on the pelvis during walking

Common injuries/symptoms: back pain, soreness, tightness, knots

Common causes: lifting without keeping back erect, lifting without keeping knees bent, lifting while holding an object too far in front of the body

*Erector Spinae Group

Notes:

Spinalis

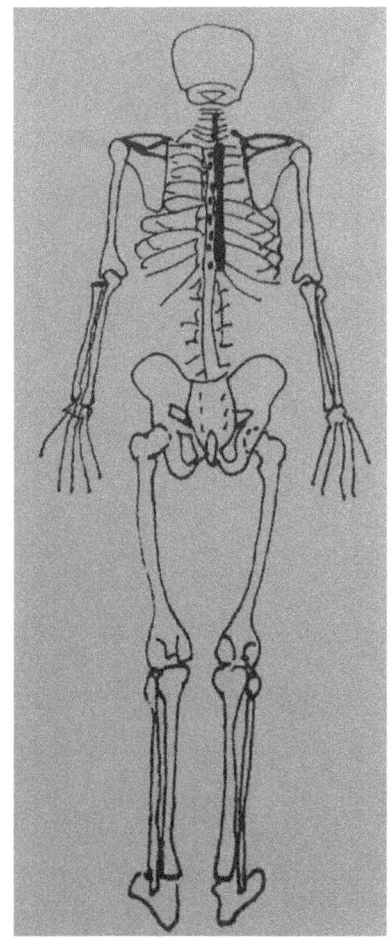

Muscle Name: *Iliocostalis

Attachments:

O-Sacrum, Iliac Crest

I - Transverse Process Cervical, Ribs

Action:

See Spinalis

Common injuries/symptoms: See spinalis

Common injuries/symptoms: See spinalis

*Erector Spinae Group

Notes:

Iliocostalis

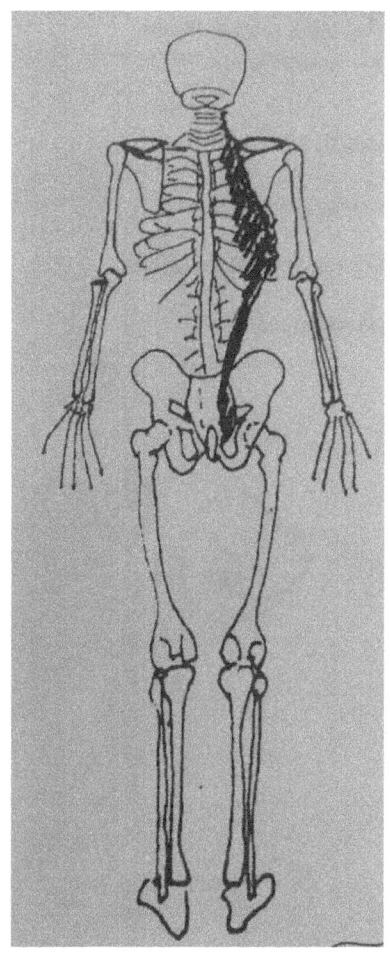

Muscle Name: *Longissimus

Attachments:

O-Sacrum, Iliac Crest, Transverse Process of Cervical,

Thoracic and Lumbar Spine I- Ribs, Transverse Processes Cervical Spine and Occiput

Action:

See Spinalis

Common injuries/symptoms: See spinalis

Common causes: see Spinalis

*Erector Spinae Group

Notes:

Longissimus

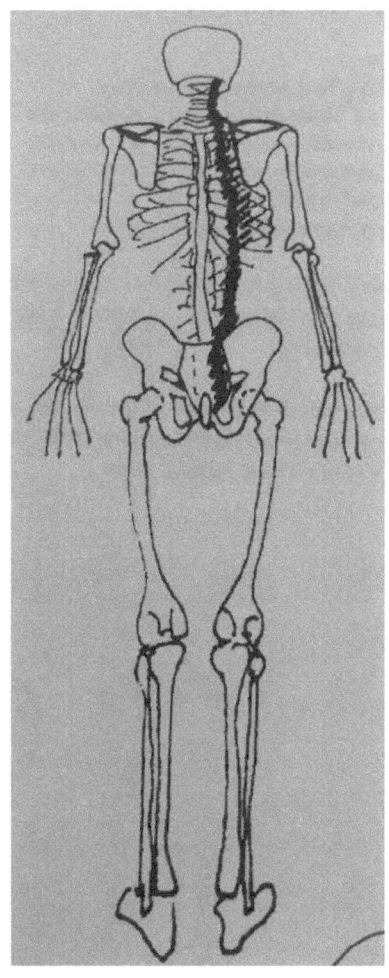

Muscle Name: Quadratus Lumborum

Attachments:

O-Iliac Crest

I-12TH Rib, Transverse Processes L1 - L4

Action:

Laterally flex the vertebral column

Fixes 12th Rib during deep respiration

Helps stabilize the diaphragm for singers

Helps extend the lumbar part of the vertebral column

giving lateral stability

Use this muscle for sitting

Common injuries/symptoms: pain, soreness, tenderness, tightness, knotting, refer pain to hip, glutes, low back area, kidney, and legs.

Common causes: prolonged driving, sitting on thick wallet, crossing legs, restricted fascia from latissimus, using muscle to lift rather than bend knees

Notes:

Quadratus Lumborum

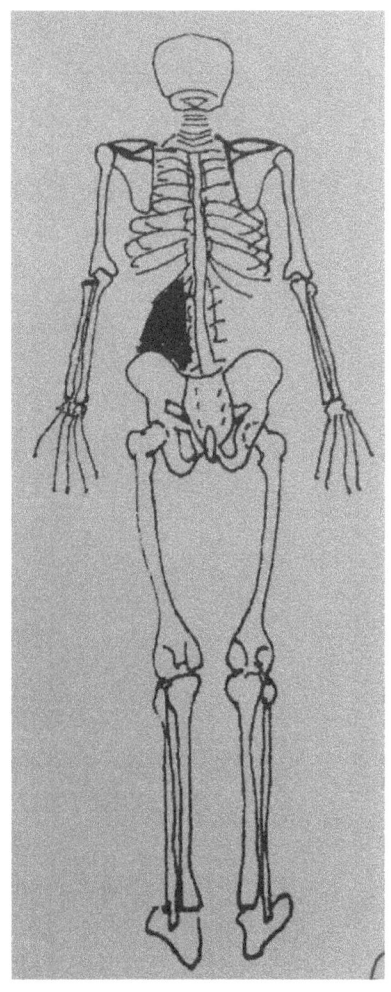

Val Nardo

HIP

GLUTEUS MINIMUS

GLUTEUS MEDIUS

GLUTEUS MAXIMUS

TENSOR FASCIA LATA

ILIOTIBIAL BAND

PIRIFORMIS

Muscle Name: Gluteus Minimus

Attachments:

O-Middle of the outer surface of Ilium

I- Anterior Border Greater Trochanter of Femur

Action:

Abducts and medially rotates hip

Common injuries/symptoms: hip pain, tightness in glut area, lower back and possibly knee pain, pelvic imbalance, limp

Common causes: sitting on a thick wallet, sudden fall, strenuous aerobic activity, standing on one foot for a long time, playing a long tennis match

Notes:

Gluteus Minimus

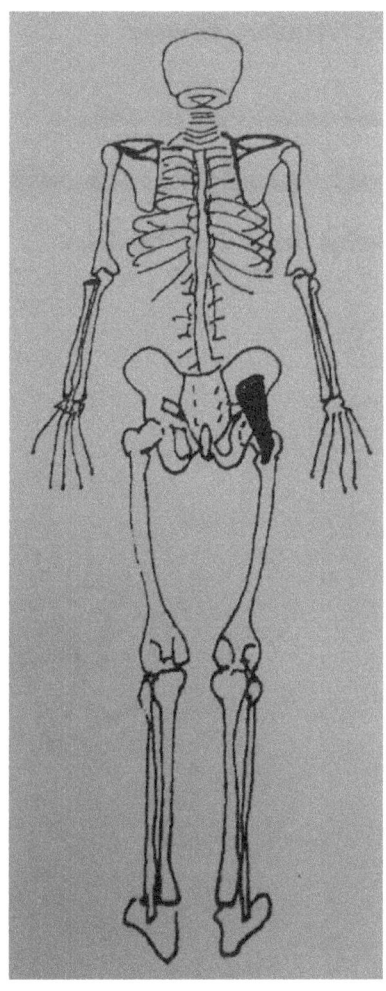

Muscle Name: Gluteus Medius

Attachments:

O-Iliac Crest

I- Greater Trochanter of Femur

Action:

Abduction and medial rotation of the femur

Common injuries/symptoms: see Gluteus Minimus

Common causes: see Gluteus Minimus

Notes:

Gluteus Medius

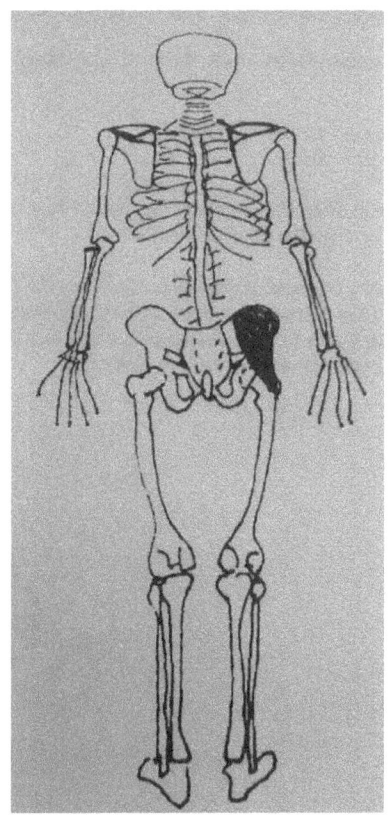

Muscle Name: Gluteus Maximus

Attachments:

O- Posterior Sacrum, Ilium, Superior Gluteal Line of Ilium

I - Gluteal Tuberosity Femur and Iliotibial Band

Action:

Extension of the femur at hip Lateral rotation of extended hip

Common injuries/symptoms: pain in gluts area and in ITB, stiffness, tightness, tenderness

Common causes: jumping, running, forceful exertion of the hip, acute stress overload during fall, prolonged walking uphill, wearing high heels, sustained vigorous lengthening of muscle, contraction in effort to prevent fall

Notes:

Gluteus Maximus

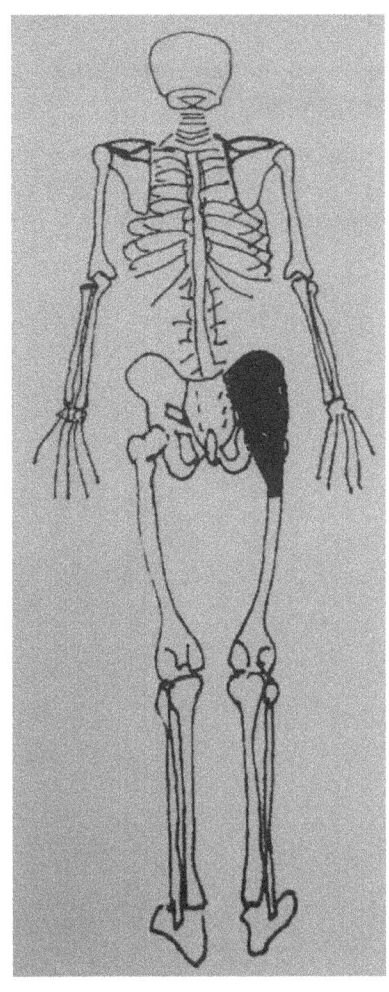

Muscle Name: Tensor Fascia Lata

Attachments:

O-Iliac Crest

I-ITB and continues to the lateral Condyle of Tibia

Action:

Flexes, abducts and medially rotates hip Stabilizes knee during walking

Common injuries/symptoms: see Gluteus Minimus

Common causes: see Gluteus Minimus

Notes:

Tensor Fascia Lata

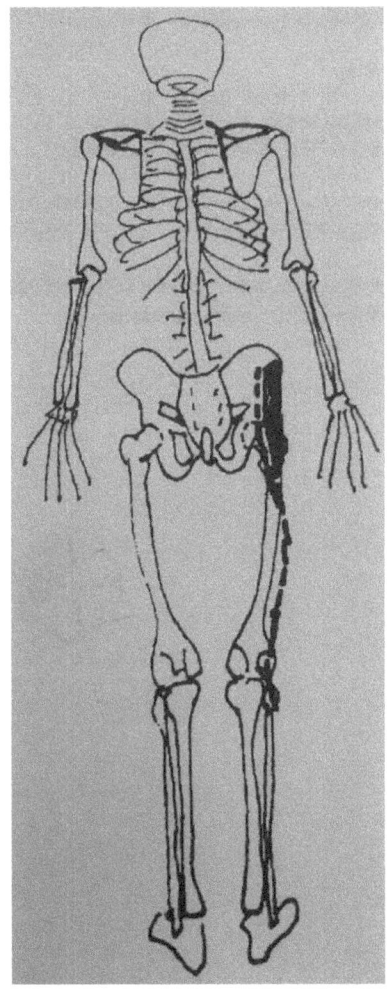

Muscle Name: Piriformis

Attachments:

O-Internal surface of Sacrum

I - Greater Trochanter of Femur

Action:

Laterally rotates hip joint and Abducts thigh when hip flexed. Helps to stabilize the femur hip socket.

Common injuries/symptoms: piriformis syndrome (sciatic pain), which begins in the buttocks area

Common causes: hypertonic muscle may squeeze the sciatic nerve (occupies same space)

Notes:

Piriformis

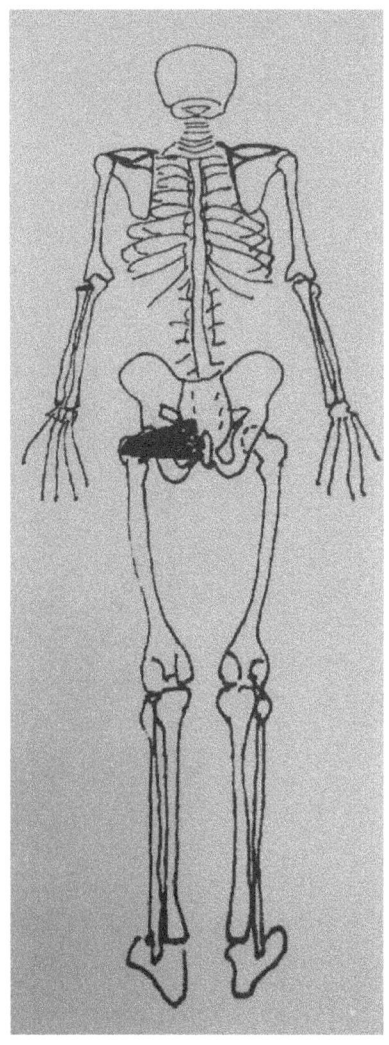

Val Nardo

THIGH (Posterior Hamstrings)

BICEPS FEMORIS

SEMIMEMBRANOSUS

SEMITENDINOSUS

Muscle Name: Biceps Femoris

Attachments:

O - Ischial Tuberosity (Sits Bone)

Posterior of Femur Linea Aspera

I- Head of Fibula

Action:

Long Head - an extension of the hip

Both Heads - flex knee and lateral rotation of flexed knee

Common injuries/symptoms: low back pain, knee pain, leg length differences, restricted walking and running stride, inability to touch toes

Common causes: overuse or misuse in sports, leisure, and working activities, shortened hamstrings, sudden lengthening of muscle without sufficient warm-up

Notes:

Biceps Femoris

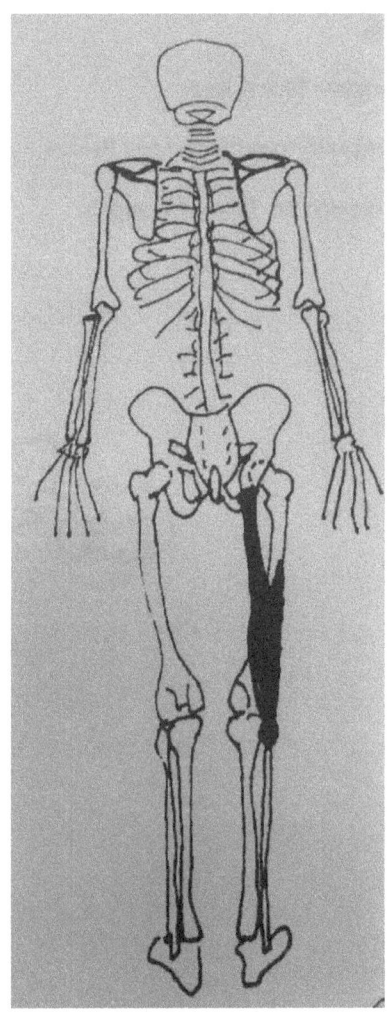

Muscle Name: Semimembranosus

Attachments:

O - Ischial Tuberosity

I - Posterior Medial Tibial Condye

Action:

Extend hip

Flex knee

Medially rotate flexed knee

Common injuries/symptoms: see Biceps Femoris

Common causes: see Biceps Femoris

Notes:

Semimembranosus

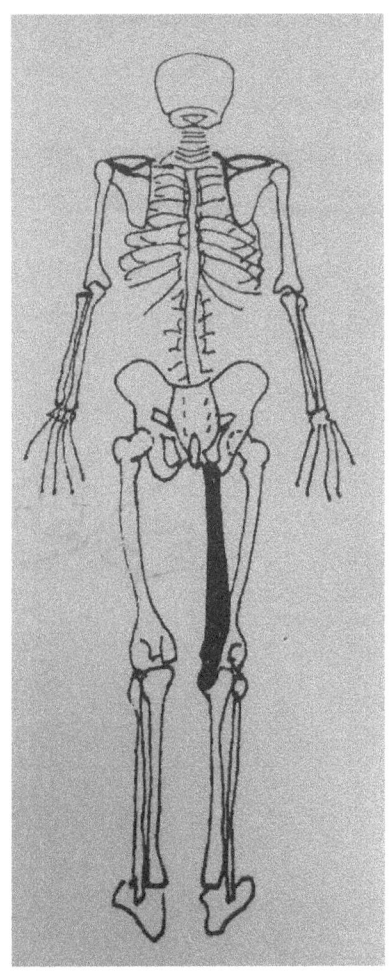

Muscle Name: Semitendinosus

Attachments:

O-Ischial Tuberosity

I - Anterior Proximal Tibial Shaft

Action:

See Rectus Femoris

Common injuries/symptoms: see Biceps Femoris

Common causes: Biceps Femoris

Notes:

Semitendinosus

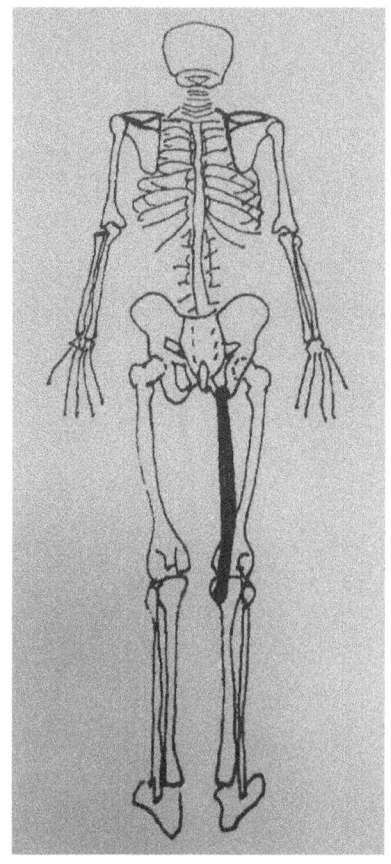

Val Nardo

THIGH (Anterior Quadraceps)

RECTUS FEMORIS

VASTUS MEDIALIS

VASTUS LATERALIS

VASTUS INTERMEDIUS

Muscle Name: Rectus Femoris

Attachments:

O-Long Head - Anterior Inferior Iliac Spine Short Head - Upper Margin of Acetabulum

I - Patella and Via Patellar Ligament to Tibial Tuberosity

Action;

Extension of knee

Assists flexion of the femur at the hip

Common injuries/symptoms: low back pain, knee pain, knee instability if muscles are tight

Common causes: overexertion in activities of sports, leisure, work, riding a motorcycle, horse riding, wave running, walking on an incline or hill that is steep

Notes:

Rectus Femoris

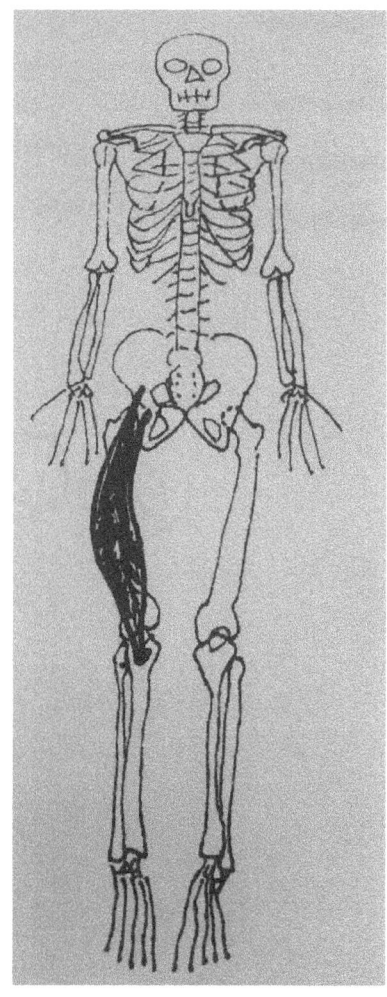

Muscle Name: Vastus Medialis

Attachments:

O-Linea Aspera on Posterior Femur

I - Petella and Via Patellar Ligament to Tibial Tuberosity

Action:

Extension of knee

Common injuries/symptoms: see Rectus Femoris

Common causes: see Rectus Femoris

Notes:

Vastus Medialis

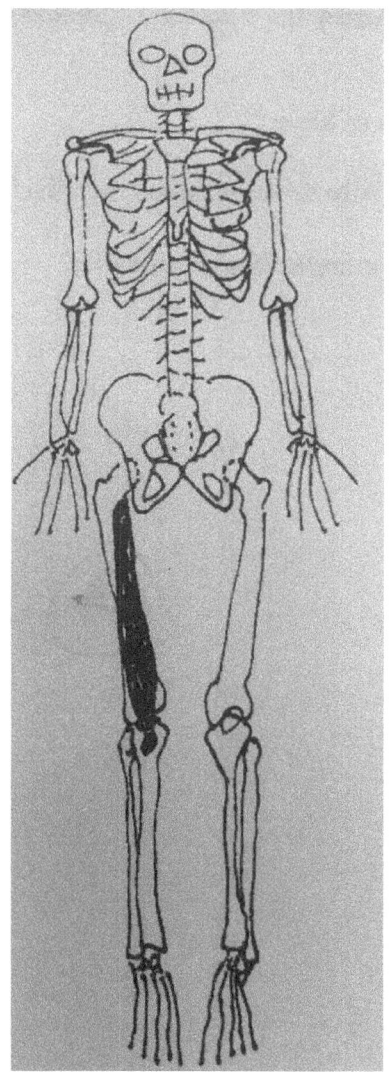

Muscle Name: Vastus Lateralis

Attachments:

O-Linea Aspera on Posterior Femur and Greater Trochanter of Femur I - Patella and Via Patellar Ligament to Tibial Tuberosity

Action:

Extension of knee

Common injuries/symptoms: see Rectus Femoris

Common causes: Rectus Femoris

Notes:

Vastus Lateralis

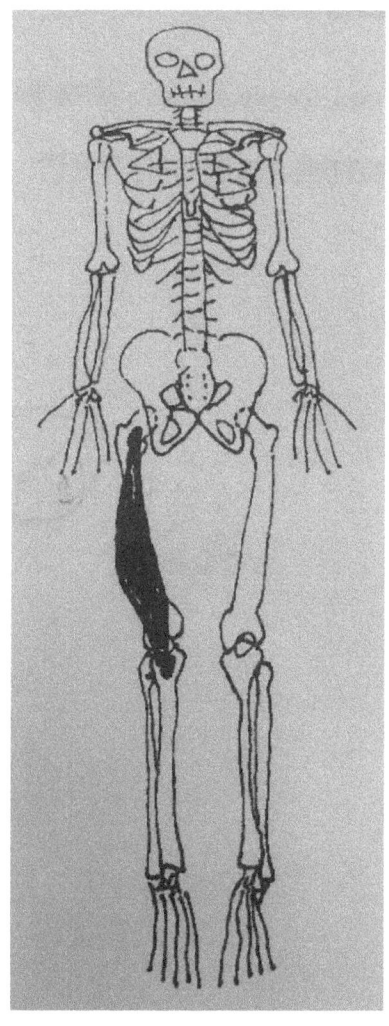

Muscle Name: Vastus Intermedialis

Attachments:

O- Anterior and Lateral Femoral Shaft

I - Patella and Via Patella Ligament to Tibial Tuberosity

Action:

Common injuries/symptoms: see Rectus Femoris

Common causes: see Rectus Remoris

Notes:

Vastus Intermedialis

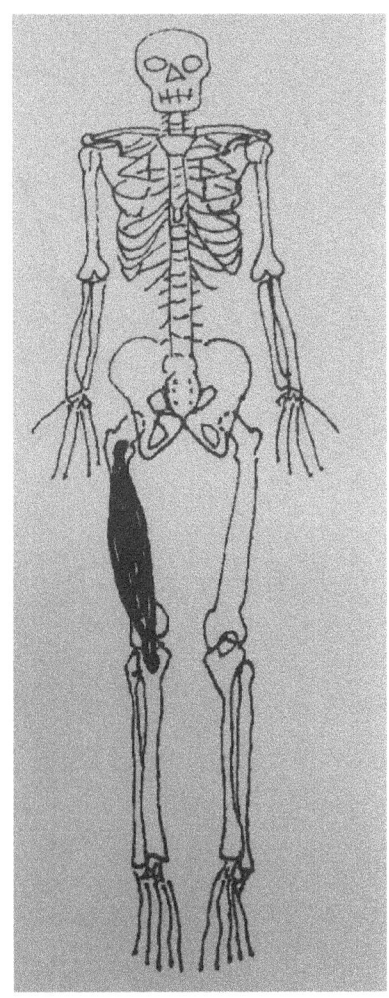

Val Nardo

LEG

PERONEALS

GASTROCNEMIUS

SOLEUS

Muscle Name: Peroneals

Attachments:

O-Longus - Upper 2/3rd of Lateral Surface of Fibula Brevis - Lower 2/3rd of Lateral Surface of Fibula I - Longus - Base of 1st Metatarsal Brevis - Base of 4th Metatarsal

Action:

Everts's foot Assists with plantar flexion of the ankle

Common injuries/symptoms: sprain or strained ankle

Common causes: forced inversion of ankle, over-stretching lateral aspect of ankle

Notes:

Peroneals

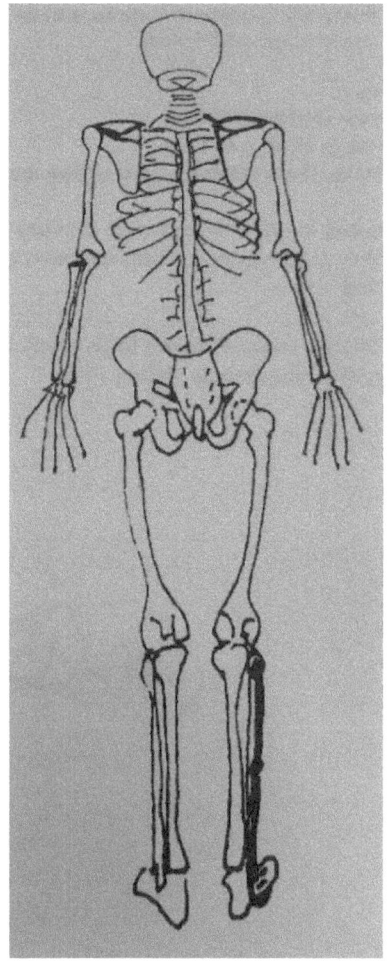

Muscle Name: Gastrocnemius

O-Medial Head - Posterior Surface of Femur above Medial Condyle

Lateral Head - Lateral Condyle and Lower Surface of Femur

I- Posterior Surface of Calcaneous into Achilles Tendon Fusion of Gastrocnemius and Soleus

Action:

Plantar flexion ankle

Assists in flexion of the knee

Maintain forward force in walking and running

Common injuries/symptoms: rupture of tendocalcaneous, Achilles Heel, very painful. Strain/strain. Posture may be affected.

Common causes: wearing high heels, landing hard from a high jump, wearing poorly fitting shoes

Notes:

Gastrocnemius

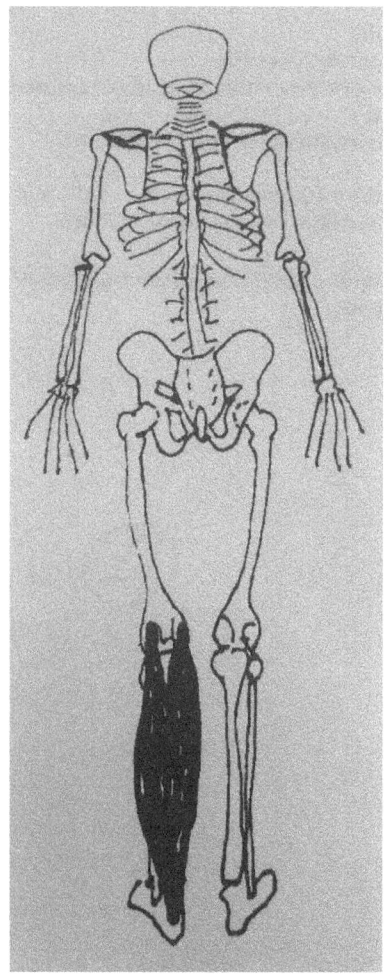

Muscle Name: Soleus

Attachments:

O-Upper Posterior Surface of Tibia and Fibula

I-With Gastrocnemius by Calcaneal Tendon

Action:

Plantar flexes ankle in contraction while standing to prevent falling forward at Ankle Helps to maintain upright posture

Common injuries/symptoms: tight and painful calves and Achilles Tendon, poor posture

Common causes: constant wearing of high heels - muscle becomes shortened

Notes:

Soleus

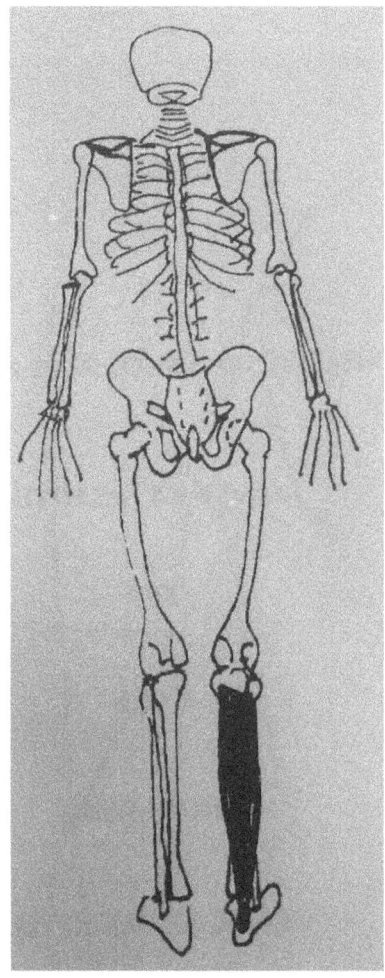

Summary
Notes for Jin Mo Qi Gong

It's important that we reiterate the principles that are illustrated above. Remember that this whole process started out as deep tissue massage. My process for deep tissue massage changed and eventually became **JIN MO QI GONG,** working with the body's fascia and energy. This theory and the process are based on the following:

*The most predominant tissue in the body is the fascia,

*Fascia's primary functions are to provide shape or form (structure) and protection,

*Fascia is everywhere in the body, around blood vessels, lymphatic tissue, nerves, muscles, literally everything in the body, even cells,

*This concept implies that, in order to affect these organs, you have to go to the fascia,

*When fascia protects, its state is at some level of constriction – this is how it protects,

*The more protection that is needed, the greater the constriction that is present,

*What is the fascia protecting the body from creating this constriction? – trauma, stress, injury, disease, overuse, just to mention a few,

*What happens when the constriction takes place in the fascia system - blood, lymph, nerves, and energy slow down functionally, and consequently, we may have pain, inflammation, and immobility. In Eastern medicine, this is called imbalance, and in Western medicine, it is called the lack of homeostasis, presenting many of the issues seen in massage offices on a daily basis,

*As a massage therapist, the most logical way to approach this problem is to focus on the tissue that is creating the problem – the fascia,

*Release tension in the fascia, and we will release the blockage in the circulatory system, lymphatic system, nervous system, and meridian system - these systems must keep flowing for an optimal state of homeostasis,

*In doing this, we provide nourishment and oxygen through the circulatory system to the muscles and organs, cleansing of toxins by way of the lymphatic system, mobility with the nervous system, and energy with the meridian system,

*This is when and how **JIN MO QI GONG** becomes relevant in the massage treatment process,

*It is important in this process that we focus on the fascia; however, it is just as, if not more important, __how__ we apply this treatment to the fascia,

*Fascia can be an extremely tough and/or rigid tissue, especially when it is in a high-level protective mode – on the other hand, it can be supple and lucid when it is in an ideal balanced state – 60% water and 40% other – normal holding state,

*Keep in mind that fascia is in constant flux, depending on those things we ask the body to do, how we stand, sit, walk, run, walk, swing at any given moment,

*Fascia has 10 times more nerve endings than muscle – it is extremely sensitive to help it make the instantaneous and numerous changes it must make on a daily basis,

*The bottom line is this – fascia has a job to do, and it will do this job at all costs, sometimes holding the tissue too long and too tight, as a mother may do with a child, possibly causing pain and discomfort. The mother will protect the child at all costs and the fascia does the same regarding the body. This is why I call the fascia "the mother of the body,"

*What is the most effective and safe way to get the fascia back in balance, given this protection function? TRUST!!!

*When the mother begins to trust the situation that caused the protection mode to take place, she will release the tightness or hold on the child, and both will begin to feel safe – likewise, the fascia will respond the same, releasing the constriction on the protected tissue, promoting trust and consequently healing,

*In order to gain this trust with the fascia, we must treat it in a non-aggressive, light manner - hence, the Sean Riehl principle regarding deep tissue massage: "No pain, work the tissue with ease, patience, sensitivity, and presence,"

*Ease – work your way into the tissue, lightly at first and adding pressure as needed, always making sure to work within a tolerable comfort range,

*Patience - promotes relaxation and awareness of change in your being and in the client's patient's being – work slowly and deliberately,

*Sensitivity - provides the ability to feel the changes taking place in the tissue so that you will be able to make necessary changes in your delivery,

*Presence - is being mindful and at the moment –it's a good idea that we start with this element since it sets the tone for the entire process - if done with proper intention, you will obtain optimal results,

*Work from your core while using your body to generate and transfer the energy that is needed into your hands and fingers, which will be relaxed and supple,

*If you focus on working with the fascia, energy, and core of your body, you will be able to achieve safe and effective results for both you and your patient/client,

*An easy and effective way to work with the core and the body for safe and effective massage application is to emulate Tai Chi and Qi Gong movement – samples can be found easily on the internet, as well as earlier in this book, **JIN MO QI GONG**

Quick and Simple Reminders

-Focus on what you are doing in the moment, presence and mindfulness,

-Be relaxed and aware,

-Use the core of your body where the energy is generated,

-the neck, shoulders, arms, wrists, hands, and fingers should be the receivers of the energy and not the generators,

-Be with the tissue that you are working with,

-Promote trust,

-Let the body do its job of natural healing – you may be witness,

-Know that the energy will go where needed without any real effort on your part,

-Research and study the concepts of energy and fascia – it will help the process be successful,

Summary

This all started with a teaching assignment that I was reluctant to accept. After accepting the assignment, I became concerned that there really was not a great deal of literature on the DTM subject, and what was there was not reliable. The assignment was Deep Tissue Massage. In short, my initial findings were that Deep Tissue Massage is, at best, a vague term. It was commonly agreed that pain and effort were needed for DTM to be effective; there was no standard protocol for DTM, and we really do not know where it came from, who originated it, or when it was born. Given this, I was still willing to pursue the assignment. The question now became, "How do we make this modality safe and effective?" My first thoughts were to go in light, take our time, and feel the tissue. There was nothing in the literature to back up this approach for accepted DTM. However, I proceeded anyway. The techniques that I developed worked in my practice, in the DTM course demonstrations, and in the course labs.

My personal petition to the universe rendered a timely and remarkable find. Six months into the program's presentations, an article by Sean Riehl, who had written for Massage Magazine, appeared in Massage Magazine, providing validation for my approach to DTM. This is what he said, "The essence of deep tissue massage is not pain, and it is not effort. It is ease, patience, sensitivity, and presence." Now I have my answer, and it is a good start. It was just the beginning. Now, many concepts have begun to fall into place very quickly. It was at this point that I began to think about calling DTM something else. Something that actually incorporated the ideas that I was promoting. What are some of these ideas? Well, we have fascia, my original DTM presentation of the concept of mindfulness, the core, safe and effective approach, Sean Riehl's statement regarding DTM, and energy, for starters. The grand scheme of things all started with Mr. Riehl's article. He quickly took pain and effort off the table. This process should not hurt your patient/client or you, and you should not have to put a lot of pressure on your application. So far, so good. It will look like this: ease, patience, sensitivity and presence.

My treatment protocol was now verified and labeled. It was no longer conventional DTM and, in some respects, took on elements of an energy technique. Why not? I always thought the two should work together. Now, I needed to take a look at why this technique worked. It turned out that this question was easily answered. It was simple: fascia. I know it is standard procedure for massage therapists to go after the muscle and what might be hurting it. However, let us take an honest look at what is really going on here. In order to get to the muscle, we really need to go through the fascia. What is involved with the fascia? Well, first of all, it is everywhere, from the outermost to innermost regions of the body. It is seamless from head to toe, in and around everything: organ, muscle, vessel, and cell in the body. It is normally 60% water and 40% ground material (elastin and collagen). It is considered to be the body's self-contained communications grid. Fascia has ten times more nerve reception than muscle. Fascia has a tensile strength in both directions of 2,000 lbs. psi. Fascia holds us together and keeps everything in its place. Fascia is the body's primary protective tissue, and for this reason, I call it The Mother of the Body. It is also why massage therapists and body workers are needed. However, only if they perform their functions properly.

Back to Riehl's theory. What we are really attempting to do is affect the muscle, and unless we can remove the fascia, this is not going to happen. So, let us work with the fascia and not against it. Riehl's suggestions fit right in here: no pain, no effort, ease, patience, sensitivity, and presence. I will quickly review how these suggestions are executed. Ease – enter the tissue (FASCIA) lightly or moderately. Fascia responds positively and quickly to this non-aggressive approach. This will begin to open up the flow systems and start the blood, lymph, and electricity to move freely, providing the muscle with what it needs to function normally. Patience is simply working slowly as you blend with the tissue change of your client. Sensitivity is being able to feel, in the most optimal way, with the primary natural tools you have: your hands. They must be soft and not involved in producing the energy needed to complete the task of the massage technique. How do we get soft hands? We bring the energy up from our core. The core is the foundation of all of our movement, large and small. If we use the muscles of our body to make that move, we waste energy and become fatigued in that area very quickly, also running the risk of injury for ourselves and our patients/clients.

Speaking of energy, I would be remiss if I did not make that connection here. All of this stuff is happening only because of energy. The atoms respond to everything we do, and energy does not demand a lot of manipulation. Actually, it takes very little to nudge the energy in a specific direction. If it is supposed to go where you want it to go, then it will. Good intention is all you need. It's that simple. All of this can be initiated by the last word in Sean Riehl's statement, which is presence, and my word is (mindfulness). Be with what you are doing in the most optimal way. It will help strengthen your intent, drive the energy, and enhance the healing process. We, as massage therapists, get to witness the whole thing. This seems to be quantum physics at its best; if observed, it is real. I leave you with that thought. P.S. note: Since this DTM concept seemed to change considerably over the seven-year period of my presentations, I felt it only appropriate to give it a new name that would include its most important elements, hence, JIN MO QI GONG.

If you adhere to the principles of working with the body's fascia and energy, produce the power needed through the core to perform the JMQG massage technique, and apply the four key words, ease, patience, sensitivity, and presence, you will be able to deliver a safe and effective service that will be as deep as it needs to be.

Epilogue

ON HEALING

In Dr. Andrew Weil's book, Spontaneous Healing, he expounds on the concept of the body's ability to heal itself. It is worth reading. I have for many years held true to this belief. This is not the way the allopathic folks look at healing. Again, Dr. Weil makes an excellent comparison of allopathic and non-traditional medical approaches. The reason I want to talk about healing is because, as massage therapists, we can not claim the ability to heal or cure a condition. I agree completely with this premise. Given this, we must establish the real source of healing. For this, I turn to Dr. Weil. He basically states the body has its own mechanisms for healing, and in many cases, if we get out of the way, it will be most effective. Again, I agree wholeheartedly. How does this affect the value of a massage therapist or any medical practitioner, for that matter, other than an M.D. or O.D.? Regarding the concept of healing, basically, no diagnosing and no prescribing. This falls in line with the FDA premise that, legitimately, the only two ways you can claim a cure is with drugs and /or surgery. Voila! M.D.s, O.D.s.

If we accept the theory that healing takes place in the body, having its own mechanisms for healing itself, then it really does not matter what initials you have after your name. The only thing any of us can really do regarding the healing process is to have an influence on it, nothing more. How does this work? If we look at the medical elements of almost any society in the world, whether it answers to a shaman or a brain surgeon, there is one factor in common that must exist in order to render the healing system optimally effective, and that is "trust." This means trust both ways, patient-practitioner and practitioner-patient. What we will realize when these partnerships begin to exist is that the healing is already working for one simple reason, "relaxation." Yes, trust promotes relaxation, and relaxation is key to the healing process. When we are relaxed, we are in the parasympathetic state, and we must be in this state for healing to take place. For example, when we sleep, we are in a parasympathetic state; we are relaxed optimally, hopefully, so the body can heal and rejuvenate itself for the next day's activity. It detoxes, it feeds, it replaces, it rebuilds, just to mention a few critical life-maintaining activities. In order for this healing process to be at an optimal level, our body must be in an optimal relaxation state. The formula looks like this, "Trust + Relaxation = Healing." No matter what the FDA may proclaim, healing can only take place primarily in and by the body. The bottom line is we, as massage therapists or any other medically related practitioner, for that matter, can only offer assistance and/or have an influence on the healing process. Trust is the main element that gives energy to this event. I offer you

JIN MO QI GONG

Bibliography

Armstrong, Colin, D.O.; Giumberteau, J-C, (2015), <u>Architecture of Human Living Fascia</u>, Handspring Publishing, United Kingdom.

Beck, Mark F. (2006). <u>Theory & Practice of Therapeutic Massage</u>, 4th ed. New York: Thompson-Delman Learning.

Biel, A. (2005). <u>The Trail Guide to the Body</u>, 3rd ed. Colorado: Books of Discovery.

Cohen, Don, (1995), <u>An Introduction to Craniosacral Therapy</u>, North Atlantic Books, California.

Cohen Danny, (1992), <u>Qi Gong Chinese Movement & Meditation for Health</u>, Wieser Books, Books, New York.

Eden, Donna, (1999), <u>Energy Medicine</u>, Tarcher Putnam, New York.

Fraser, Peter; Massey, Harry, (2008), <u>Decoding the Human Body Field</u>, Healing Arts Press, Rochester.

Gerber, Richard, M.D., (2001), <u>Vibrational Medicine</u>, Bear & Company, Rochester.

Ingber, D.E., (2008), <u>Tensegrity and Mechanotransduction</u>, Journal of Bodywork and Movement Therapies, Vol: 12 198-200

Jarmey, C, (2003), <u>The Concise Book of Muscles</u>, North Atlantic Books, California.

McTaggart, Lynne, (2002), <u>The Field</u>, Harper Perennial, New York.

Muscolino, D.C., (2010), <u>Body Mechanics, Seven Keys To Healthy Neck Posture</u>, Massage Therapy Journal, Spring vol 49(1) 93-97.

Ried, Daniel, (2000), <u>The Complete Guide To Chi-Gung</u>, Shambhala, Boston.

Riggs, Art, (2007), <u>Deep Tissue Massage-A Visual Guide To Techniques</u>, North Atlantic Books Rev. ed, California.

Wiel, Andrew, M.D., (1996), <u>Spontaneous Healing</u>, Ballentine Books, New York.

Biography

Val Nardo, LMT, M.Ed., Ph.D., retired

Val Nardo Jr is a retired massage practitioner/educator. He practiced massage therapy from 2002 – 2016. He was a massage educator from 2005 – 2016. Dr. Nardo was a Florida LMT and was Board Certified with NCBTMB, as well as a Certified Vocational Rehabilitation Counselor. He received his massage training from the Academy of Healing Arts in Lake Worth, Florida, in 2002, an M.Ed. from Coppin State College, Baltimore, Maryland, 1972, and a Ph.D. in Natural Health from Clayton College Of Natural Health Birmingham, Alabama, 2006. Dr. Nardo received more than 200 hours of advanced training in various massage disciplines, including medical massage, craniosacral therapy, assessment of upper and lower extremities, and reiki. Dr. Nardo is a Reiki master and a Qi Gong instructor. As a massage practitioner, Dr. Nardo provided massage services for several local chiropractors and operated his own massage company. As a massage therapy educator, Dr. Nardo provided live national CEU training services for Cross Country Education and video presentations for Home CEU Connection. Dr. Nardo was also a massage instructor at Keiser University. Finally, for nearly 40 years, Dr. Nardo was a certified vocational counselor and for 30+ years served as a court vocational expert witness. Dr. Nardo's book, JIN MO QI GONG, is a transfer of information and knowledge gained while having experienced the privilege of teaching and practicing massage therapy. It is his wish that this information will inspire and open new worlds of inquiry and development for massage and related healthcare therapists.

Val Nardo

www.ingramcontent.com/pod-product-compliance
Lightning Source LLC
Chambersburg PA
CBHW051621120626
46551CB00014B/1900